Penguin Books

The Reading Bug
... and how you can help your child to catch it

Paul je   s worked as a special-education teacher, then speech pathologist, then
becam·   nior education lecturer before turning to full-time writing. Helping children
learn t·   particularly those with difficulties, has been a huge motivator throughout his   ·.

Jennin·   phenomenon in the world of children's books. Since the publication of
Unreal   ·5, he has been entertaining children of all ages with his tales of the
strang·   ne fantastic, encouraging them to become enthusiastic, skilled readers.
He has   n more than one hundred stories, and sales of his books exceed 6.7
million

His mo·   · books include *Tongue-Tied!*, his tenth book of short stories, which won the
2002 Y·   stralians Best Books Award (YABBA), and the *Rascal the Dragon* series, four
brilliant   ·le books for beginner readers. He is also the creator of the much-loved
Singen·   d Gizmo books, and the co-creator (with Morris Gleitzman) of the best-selling
s·   ·ls, *Wicked!* and *Deadly!*. The top-rating TV series 'Round the Twist' is based
c   of his enormously popular stories.

BOOKS BY PAUL JENNINGS

Unreal!
Unbelievable!
Quirky Tails!
Uncanny!
Unbearable!
Unmentionable!
Undone!
Uncovered!
Unseen!
Thirteen Unpredictable Tales
Tongue-Tied!

The Cabbage Patch Fib
The Cabbage Patch War
The Cabbage Patch Pong

The Gizmo
The Gizmo Again
Come Back Gizmo

The Paw Thing

Sucked In . . .
(illustrated by Terry Denton)

Totally Wicked!
Deadly! (series)
(with Morris Gleitzman)

Spit it Out!
(with Terry Denton and Ted Greenwood)

The Reading Bug

Rascal the Dragon
Rascal in Trouble
Rascal Takes Off
Rascal's Trick

PICTURE BOOKS

The Fisherman and the Theefyspray
(illustrated by Jane Tanner)

The Reading Bug
. . . and how you can help your child to catch it

Paul Jennings

Illustrations by

Andrew Welden.

PENGUIN BOOKS

Published by the Penguin Group
Penguin Books Ltd, 80 Strand, London WC2R ORL, England
Penguin Group (USA), Inc., 375 Hudson Street, New York, New York 10014, USA
Penguin Books Australia Ltd, 250 Camberwell Road, Camberwell, Victoria 3124, Australia
Penguin Books Canada Ltd, 10 Alcorn Avenue, Toronto, Ontario, Canada M4V 3B2
Penguin Books India (P) Ltd, 11 Community Centre, Panchsheel Park, New Delhi – 110 017, India
Penguin Group (NZ), cnr Airborne and Rosedale Roads, Albany, Auckland 1310, New Zealand
Penguin Books (South Africa) (Pty) Ltd, 24 Sturdee Avenue, Rosebank 2196, South Africa

Penguin Books Ltd, Registered Offices: 80 Strand, London WC2R ORL, England

www.penguin.com

First published by Penguin Books Australia Ltd, 2003
Published in Penguin Books, 2004

1

Copyright © Lockley Lodge Pty Ltd, 2003
Illustrations copyright © Andrew Weldon, 2003
All rights reserved

Printed in England by Clays Ltd, St Ives plc

To my mother,
Phyllis Jane Jennings,
from whom I caught the reading bug.

THANK YOU

All the books in the text of *The Reading Bug* are my personal recommendations. For the wider list and the scrutiny of my manuscript I am indebted to Kerry White, who made frequent use of The Source at *www.magpies.net.au*, Penny Forth, Moira Robinson, Kay Sagar and Wendy Cooling. These five people between them have immeasurable knowledge of children and books. I cannot thank them enough for their assistance.

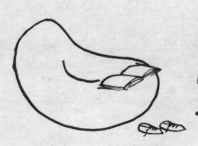

SHE GOT LOST IN A BOOK— THAT WAS A WEEK AGO...

IN THIS BOOK

<table>
<tr><td></td><td>THANK YOU</td><td>x</td></tr>
<tr><td></td><td>YOU ARE IT</td><td>xi</td></tr>
<tr><td>1</td><td>**Become an Expert**
It's not brain surgery</td><td>1</td></tr>
<tr><td>2</td><td>**Reading to Children**
A lifelong love affair</td><td>13</td></tr>
<tr><td>3</td><td>**Matching Children and Books**
What they want is what they need</td><td>31</td></tr>
<tr><td>4</td><td>**The Importance of Stories**
Joining the human race</td><td>51</td></tr>
</table>

<table>
<tr><td>5</td><td>**Preschool and Beginners**
Like the words of a song</td><td>63</td></tr>
</table>

YOU ARE IT

The Reading Bug is a guide. It is a do-it-yourself book. I am proud of this. I will be even prouder if you find it easy to read and interesting because I have done my very best to make it so.

One of the few bits of praise I received at school was when a teacher held up my history paper and said, 'Jennings has answered the question just as well as anyone else but has used only half the number of words.'

For some reason, I have always been able to get to the guts of an issue with a small number of words. When children read, they need this.

Kids may give the author a page to prove him or herself. Some will abandon a book after the first paragraph or even a single sentence. This is fair enough, and it is the reason I have listed some amazing and fascinating books for you to consider as you help them along the road to a lifelong love of reading.

I have always said that the biggest sin a children's author can commit is to be boring. Your children will be the final judge of the titles listed here. And you will be the judge of this book. You may not agree with everything I have to say. But I guarantee that you won't drown in jargon or imponderable sentences.

'Is there one single factor which indicates how well a child will do with reading when they start school?'

I put this question to a senior teacher shortly before his retirement. Without pausing to think he answered, 'The involvement of the parents.'

The purpose of this book is to involve you in your children's reading education. I hope I am successful in this. The one person who will do more than anyone else to help your children learn to read . . .

. . . is you.

Paul Jennings

1

Become an Expert

It's not brain surgery

IN THIS CHAPTER

* Anyone who can read can teach reading.
* If children love something you can't stop them doing it.
* Reading to or with a child is an act of love.
* Without a single 'lesson' they will come to love reading.
* Our goal is to instil a love, an attitude, a passion.
* We are going to create a whole-language home.

If you are a parent, you already have the major ingredient to infect a child with the reading bug – love. You love your kids and children love to be loved. Inject this into the reading situation and you will succeed. This is my main point. Love is the foundation on which we build.

It's not brain surgery

Teachers are incredibly skilled people. But these days they are asked to do so much that they cannot give all aspects of the curriculum the deserved attention. Primary school teachers are called upon to be psychologists, social workers, nurses and bookkeepers in addition to mastering the curriculum areas of music, sport, science, English, reading, spelling, mathematics, geography, art and philosophy. Each area is extremely complex and needs big slabs of time for preparation and individual

3

tuition to meet the needs of each child. It is just too much for one person to take on.

The way many governments have allowed the teaching profession to be under-funded is something that the whole community will come to regret. Investing in our children's future takes dollars but putting money into human resources is not always visible or able to be measured. Politicians prefer monuments that can be seen.

Teachers need your help

You have probably already been nominated as a reading aid or helper at your child's school. You are not there simply for economic reasons. There are great benefits to the children when they see Mum, Dad or friends involved in teaching reading. It is a great example and a sign of how much you yourself value books.

Parents are much better placed to give individual instruction than are teachers. A parent doesn't have thirty or more students to work with. The best teacher in the world can't fit thirty half-hours of reading instruction into a six-hour day. But parents can give their children half an hour of reading fun every day if they want to. Reading to or with a child is an act of love.

If you are not able to go to the school you will

undoubtedly be involved at home. Every parent is familiar with little schoolbooks known as 'readers'. It is usually the parent's task to listen to their child read aloud every night and tick off the pages to show that it's been done. On the surface there doesn't seem to be much involved in listening to reading. But there are some dos and don'ts which we examine in Chapter 5. Helping children with their reading is not difficult but you need the right techniques. When you know them it can make all the difference.

Like the old cliché – it's easy when you know how.

By the time you have finished this book you should have the guts of it.

Kids hate mush

Just after I left teachers' college at nineteen years of age I was invited to a friend's home for lunch. Being a teacher himself, he kindly gave me a few tips to start me off in my new career. I don't remember any of his advice. But I do remember something that happened.

His two-year-old son sat in a highchair between the teacher and his wife. Bowls of soup were placed in front of the adults. The infant was offered some vegetable mush on a spoon. He clenched his teeth

5

and shook his head. Instantly the father pounced. He grabbed the little boy's jaw and forced it open. Then he shoved the mush into his mouth and put the child into a headlock so that he couldn't open his jaws.

Nothing was said by any of us. Obviously this had happened before. The father ate his soup with one hand and held the child's head with the other. The roast was served – the teacher's wife cut up his food into small pieces as you would for a child. The man ate with difficulty but managed to maintain his headlock on the hapless infant. The child grew red in the face but was able to breathe through his nose.

The conversation continued without reference to this extraordinary incident. The desserts followed and then coffee. A good hour passed with the child and father locked in their silent struggle. Finally the time came for me to leave and the little boy was reluctantly released. He gasped for air and then spat the mush onto the floor.

Kids hate mush. And so do I.

Because of their own experiences as children, many parents try to teach reading as if the words, letters and sounds can be shovelled in like soggy vegetables. They can't.

This incident has always stayed in my mind as an example of a simple truth. If children don't like something, you can't make them do it – if children love something, you can't stop them. If children are to be lifelong readers, we must instil a love of books.

Nothing but fun

Our aim is not to teach decoding or sounding out or recognising words. It is to instil a love, an attitude, a passion. Right from the very beginning.

There is no room for pain. There is no room for struggle. There is no place for boredom. At this point I will come right out and say what I believe passionately after a lifetime of teaching children and writing books for them. I believe the early stages of reading should not involve any effort on the part of the child. It should be fun and nothing but fun.

A child who thinks that reading is rotten has been robbed.

I am going to avoid jargon. Complex terminology is often used to exclude everyone but those in the know. It is a way of blackballing you from the club. Good writing is easy to understand. When I was studying psychology I would come across meaningless paragraphs in a text-book. I used to feel dumb. I wasn't. The writer was.

It is not necessary to complicate new ideas with complex terminology. This is often done to elevate the

7

status of the writer. A parent can learn to teach reading without having to memorise jargon. There is no exam at the end of the course. There is just a kid lying on a bed with a book and refusing to put out the light.

In a nutshell

The modern world is so different from that of our childhood that it leaves us reeling. We ride on in-line skates not rollerskates. Our doctors use modern keyhole surgery in place of major operations. We send e-mails instead of letters. Plasma screens are replacing cathode tubes in television sets. But we approach the teaching of reading . . . *in exactly the same way our parents did.*

However, like medicine, skating and television, things have moved on. It is difficult to adapt to change and many of us want to do things the way they have always been done. This is only to be expected in the field of reading instruction. Most parents are not teachers so their major resource is their own experience.

It is unlikely that you were helped to read using many of the methods that I outline in this book. Some of the ways that you were asked to do things as a child have been discredited. Other techniques are still used but hotly debated. Many strategies have been incorporated into new approaches.

I am going to use an example to describe the basis of teaching reading recommended in this book. It is not a proof, but it describes the thrust of the approach you can use to help your children catch the reading bug. If you keep this example in the back of your mind, you will see hundreds of opportunities to help your children on their way to success with print. Without a single 'lesson' they will come to love reading.

Learning to talk. This is my example. The whole thing in a nutshell. A baby is saturated with speech and language from the day he or she is born. Parents lean over the cot murmuring loving words. We smile delightedly at the most distant approximation. 'Ga, ga,' is Daddy. It definitely is. 'Moo, moo,' is Mummy. We are sure of it. This babbling is rewarded with cuddles, laughs and approval.

We would not dream of sternly saying, 'The word is *Mother*, not *moo, moo*.' We are delighted when a rabbit is identified as a *bunny*. We praise this early effort.

The meaningless vocalisations of the baby are treasured. We know instinctively that babbling is an early stage of talking. We are totally aware that we must bathe our children in speech. We talk to them in the car and the bath. We point things out and give explanations. We listen without criticism to early vocal play. 'Daddy go,' is viewed as a wonderful step forward. It is not met with a correction like, 'Wrong, Jodie, you should say, "Daddy is leaving for work."' We may respond with, 'Yes, good girl. Daddy is leaving for work,' but we would never punish it or point out the grammatical error. We are not hung up on accuracy. Constantly correcting speech would have a negative effect. We know that after repeated exposures to speech the child will get closer and closer to the correct grammatical forms.

It is amazing how children internalise these rules. Their very mistakes are indications of their ability to internalise grammatical structures. *I climb, I climbed. I run, I runned.* How logical. How amazing.

We are going to teach reading in a similar way. We are going to bathe the children in print. We are going to accept their early ramblings as they turn the pages with delight because we know this 'yabber' is an early stage of reading in the same way that babbling is an early stage of talking. We are going to smile at their approximations.

We are going to keep quiet when our child reads *bunny* instead of *rabbit*. We are not going to be hung up on accuracy. We are not going to insist that every word and every letter be read correctly.

We are going to create a world of useful and fascinating print. We are going to praise, stimulate and accept. We are going to develop an environment in which reading will naturally occur. There will be books and magazines and papers and calendars and charts and summaries and pictures and stories everywhere.

And we are going to set the example. We are going to read ourselves. For our own benefit. It's no good trying to spread the reading bug if you haven't caught it yourself. Many teachers have a quiet reading time in which they sit at their desk and read a novel or book that interests them while the children do the same. We

11

are going to demonstrate that reading is an activity done for our own benefit, not someone else's.

In schools such an environment would be called the 'whole-language' classroom. We are going to create the whole-language home.

2

Reading to Children

A lifelong love affair

IN THIS CHAPTER

* The fun, the fears and the fellowship of a magic moment.
* A lifelong love affair.
* Supermarket rules.
* Maps, manuals and tombstones.
* The shyest person can be Billy Connolly.

'Look, it's okay for you, Dad,' says my secretary after she reads the early draft of this chapter. 'But when I leave work I have to shop, cook, feed the chickens, help two kids with their homework, do the washing, play with the baby and try to stay pleasant when I am absolutely exhausted. Plus, it would be nice now and then to find time to read a book that I like. Or see a movie. It's not easy finding time to read stories.'

Lyndu is my grown-up daughter. 'I know that,' I say. 'And the reason I know is that I helped bring up six kids and I have been through it myself.'

She grins back. We both know I have paid my dues. But I'm not feeling smug about it. I am riddled with guilt like all parents because I didn't spend enough time with the kids. Not enough time going to the park, or the movies, or helping with homework or reading stories out loud. When I think about the duties of parenthood I feel exhausted. It is tough and I sympathise with modern parents. I really do.

But reading to your children is one of the most valuable things you can do for them. If you can possibly do it, try to fit some story-reading into your busy schedule. The benefits are enormous. And not just to the children. I have to say that when I hear Lyndu read to my grandchildren from *Harry the Dirty Dog* by Gene Zion and Margaret Bloy Graham, I feel a glow of pride.

As she reads the sentence, 'Harry was a white dog with black spots,' she puts on the same voice that signals, 'But not for long,' in the same way that I did with her when she and her five brothers and sisters took turns sitting on my knee twenty-five years ago.

16

A lifelong love affair

Reading aloud to your children gives them an incredibly strong message. Without words you are saying, 'I am not washing the car or reading the paper or watching the news. I am sitting here with you, reading a story about a little dog whose family don't recognise him when he gets dirty. I am enjoying sitting in bed with you, sharing the fun, the fears and the fellowship of this magic moment. You are the centre of my world.'

And when you look down at the sparkling eyes you know beyond a shadow of a doubt that you are the centre of theirs.

This act of love forms an association between the child and books. The word *book* brings pleasure. The feel, look and smell of books is forever linked to feelings of warmth, security and love. You have started a lifelong love affair between a child and reading.

Contrast this with the child whose first experience is shame and failure as they struggle with words that contain no meaning or joy. This can happen to children whose first reading experiences are formal tasks at which they fail.

Make sure that the word *book* gets as big an emotional response as the word *birthday*. Some people read to the baby in the womb. You might find this a bit much,

17

GREAT BOOKS FOR BABIES

Playtime, Poppy Cat
a touch-and-feel book
Lara Jones

That's Not My Train
touchy-feely book
Fiona Watt and Rachel Wells

Rosie's Walk board book
Pat Hutchins

The Very Hungry Caterpillar board book
Eric Carle

Owl Babies board book
Martin Waddell, Patrick Benson (illus.)

Tickle, Tickle board book
Helen Oxenbury

The Rainbow Fish bath book
Marcus Pfister

Buggy Buddies
tiny board books to attach to a highchair, car seat, buggy – anywhere!

but certainly begin before the child can talk. Buy rag books like Disney's *Winnie the Pooh soft book* which comes with a soft toy and is suitable for babies from birth to nine months. Or buy cardboard books. Let the baby pull and rip at them.

There are hundreds of books available which are also toys. They float or have wheels. They are shaped like hamburgers or boxes. They squeak or talk. When the page is turned pictures pop out like flowers opening. Some books fold out to be a metre long. Others form themselves into mobiles which can be hung from the ceiling. There are pages that can be sniffed and others with flaps to lift. Paper dragons and monsters pounce from the pages as if alive.

These books are a fantastic introduction for littlies. Beg, borrow or deal. But get them at all costs. They may be toys but they are also a terrific turn-on to reading. They have a simple message for pre-readers – books are fun.

The language of books is learned – not taught

Reading to your child does more than create a love of books. It prepares children for their own silent reading by getting them used to the language of books.

Here's a bit of everyday modern speech. I have taken a passage from a classic story and rephrased it the way it might be uttered in the modern world:

The Queen goes, 'Get rid of that mouse.' So we
all ran around and eventually chucked it out.
By the time we calm down the cook has shot through.

19

That is how someone might describe the incident orally. This is how Lewis Carroll described it in *Alice's Adventures in Wonderland*:

> 'Collar that Dormouse!' the Queen shrieked out. 'Behead that Dormouse! Turn that Dormouse out of court! Suppress him, pinch him, off with his whiskers!'
>
> For some minutes the whole court was in confusion, getting the Dormouse turned out, and, by the time they had settled down again, the cook had disappeared.

The passage from *Alice in Wonderland* is rich, expressive and colourful but you have probably never uttered anything like it. It is the language of books, not speech. When we talk to each other we use 'ums' and 'ahs', incomplete sentences and shortcuts. The 'he saids' and 'she saids' are less numerous. In fact, listening on the train to a group of teenagers the other day I was struck by how often they use the phrase 'he goes' or 'she goes' instead of 'he said' and 'she said'.

The grammar in books is different to the grammar in speech. In the *Alice in Wonderland* passage, Lewis Carroll does not change tense halfway through the paragraph. If I accidentally did so in one of my stories my editor would correct it. If you read to children they will know about tense consistency without being able explain it. It will help them to predict when they read by themselves.

As evidence of this, I can point to a recipe a little girl made up for me. It arrived in my fan mail with twenty other pieces of creative writing from a class of primary-school children. There were stories, poems, anecdotes, autobiographical pieces and one recipe.

Here it is:

Take a mug and add warm milk. Put in a spoonful
of cocoa and add sugar to taste. Stir. It is delicious.

This little girl has obviously read or been read recipe books. She knows (unconsciously) to use present tense. She even knows that one-word sentences may be used as commands. She has learned the language of recipe books. She has probably also learned the language of storybooks, instruction manuals, poetry books, maps, tombstones and signage in supermarkets.

The child who has not been read to has missed out on internalising the various language forms of print, and is less able to predict what a passage is about. This ability is learned, not taught. That is why it is impossible to do too much reading aloud to kids.

We have all been amazed at times by very small children with incredible vocabularies who read before they go to school. They will almost certainly have been read to at home by a parent who knows the importance of exposure to the various written codes. Follow one of them around the supermarket and I will guarantee you will find a parent pointing out labels, sending the child off in search of tins, and making a reading and language game out of the whole shopping trip. The child is internalising the oral and written language of the supermarket.

An internal map

Children learn the grammar of speech because they are spoken to. They learn the language of books because they are read to. But they are two different systems and children need to be exposed to both.

When we speak we have some help that is not available in books. We emphasise particular words. When my wife saw the bleak, lonely clifftop where I wanted to build a house she said, 'I'm the only woman in the world who would live here with you.' Was the emphasis on 'here' or on 'you'? I hope it was the former. Question marks, exclamation marks and italics can indicate intonation in books but they can never match the rich variations of speech.

I think the use of exclamation marks is too convenient and I try to indicate excitement by the choice of words. I have never used an exclamation mark in a story although my publisher chose to put one on the cover of my first book. (I was really tempted to insert one at the end of that last sentence.)

In books we have punctuation marks and grammatical and genre clues which are just as critical to the reader as intonation clues are to the listener. These rules become unconsciously internalised through frequent exposure. For example, there are hundreds of ways of indicating dialogue. I usually stick to 'he said' and 'she

said' to indicate who has spoken. This might seem a little bland but it makes things easier for young readers. One of my favourite authors is the American short-story writer Raymond Carver. I read about twelve of his tales before I noticed that he only used 'he said' and 'she said' as dialogue markers.

More complicated ways of indicating a speaker are difficult to process; for example:

> She acknowledged his suggestion with the sharp
> reply, 'Get lost.'

When we read to children they become familiar with these structures and recognise them more easily when they read by themselves.

Deaf children don't learn to talk unless given special help because they do not hear the rules of language in speech. Similarly, kids will not internalise the language of books before they get to school unless they are exposed to them by adult readers. The sentences in books can be gobbledygook to children who have not been read to.

In effect, kids whose parents read to them know what to expect when they try to make sense of the written word. They have an internal map. They know the conventions. What child can't finish the phrase, 'Once upon a . . .'? Children who have heard stories can predict what an unknown word might be because they have covered this territory before. We are helping the children to guess based on their experience. And as we shall see later, guessing is good – because it really isn't guessing at all.

Another obvious benefit from reading to your children is the increase in the number of words that they know. In *The Tale of the Flopsy Bunnies*, Beatrix Potter writes, 'They were feeling quite soporific.' I first came across the word *soporific* when I was an adult and had to look it up in the dictionary. How wonderful when a child says, 'What does that mean, Dad?' The child is learning without knowing it.

It's not fair to leave it all up to teachers. And anyway the critical years are not in teachers' hands. By the time kids reach kindergarten we have had wonderful opportunities for reading aloud. Grandparents, childminders and friends can be encouraged to join in the fun. Leave some favourite books in their homes as resources. If you have a partner, share the reading. Dads and mums who don't participate in this are letting the side down.

And they are missing out themselves. A good children's book always has something to please an adult as well. You can choose a book like *The Hobbit* by J.R.R. Tolkien which is an adult tale quite suitable for children of eleven or twelve if someone reads it to them.

Carrots not sticks

Put aside a special time of the day when you won't be interrupted. Bedtime is good because the children will look forward to the story. You can get them into their pyjamas with their teeth cleaned because a reward is coming. Then at the end you can turn off the light and have a little time to yourself.

'This is all very well,' I hear you say. 'But my son or daughter won't get off the computer. And I can't drag them away from the television.'

There is no easy answer to this problem. But there are some commonsense strategies we can employ. Firstly, storytime does not need to happen instead of some other pleasurable activity. It should be a bonus rather than a punishment. Don't drag the child from the television. Rather,

GREAT BOOKS FOR PARENTS TO READ ALOUD

Babies
That's Not My Bear . . . a touchy-feel book
Fiona Watt, Rachel Wells (illus.)

Pre-school
The Man Whose Mother Was a Pirate
Margaret Mahy

Infants
I Will Not Ever, NEVER, Eat a Tomato
Lauren Child

Primary
The Witches
Roald Dahl, Quentin Blake (illus.)

A Wizard of Earthsea
Ursula le Guin, Ruth Robbins (illus.)

Love That Dog
Sharon Creech

Time Stops for No Mouse
Michael Hoeye

Secondary
Holes
Louis Sachar

The Illustrated Mum
Jacqueline Wilson, Nick Sharratt (illus.)

have a set bedtime. Then, as a reward, a story may be offered instead of having the light off. In this way the child perceives the story as something to be gained rather than lost. It is a carrot not a stick.

It is quite reasonable to set limits on television and computer games. Most parents require children to do jobs and homework as well as spend some time playing games and getting outside if at all possible. Few allow uncontrolled viewing.

When should you stop reading aloud to your children? There is no one answer but they will usually tell you when they feel they don't need it any more. In my own

family we have stopped at eight or nine years of age with a child who just wanted to read to themselves. Others have still been enjoying a bedtime story when they are fourteen. I still like to be read to.

Audio tapes

There is no substitute for the parent or caregiver reading to a child. Audio tapes, however, are extremely useful as aids to storytelling and often have added features like sound effects or the voice of the author narrating. Unlike television, the imagination is required to visualise the tale. And the language structures are the same as in books because the words are not altered. Some top titles like *Goodnight Mister Tom* by Michelle Magorian are readily available. Nearly all of my own stories are on audio tapes.

You have probably discovered that a particularly good place to use tapes is in the car. When a journey is long and the children are restless, an audio book can give

GREAT STORIES ON AUDIO TAPE

Pre-school and infants

Spot's Bedtime Storybook
Eric Hill

Angelina Ballerina's Story Collection
Katherine Holabird, Helen Craig (illus.)

Six Storey House
Geraldine McCaughrean

The Enormous Crocodile
Roald Dahl

Primary

Mr Majeika
Humphrey Carpenter

Judy Moody Gets Famous
Megan McDonald

A Series of Unfortunate Events
Lemony Snicket

Top Primary/Secondary

The Wind Singer
William Nicholson

29

pleasure to the whole family as well as being of great value in building the language skills that underpin reading.

What is the most important thing you can do to help your child's reading skills? If pressed, I would have to say reading aloud to a child from a very early age is the most beneficial thing you can do.

And really ham it up. The shyest person can become Billy Connolly in the privacy of a child's bedroom. Put on voices, roll your eyes, whisper in fear. Whoop and jump around. You are a dragon, a princess or a king.

If you would like to know more about reading to your young children, Dorothy Butler's excellent *Babies Need Books* is devoted to this topic.

3

Matching Children and Books

What they want is what they need

IN THIS CHAPTER

* What they want is what they need.
* The look of a book is incredibly important.
* There is no such thing as a book for reluctant readers.
* Keep personality characteristics in mind.
* You need a top story.
* An easy-to-read book can be wonderful.
* Judging reading levels.
* Fashions have changed.

My first book launch in 1985 was a big occasion for me. All my friends came to Warrnambool Books, our local educational bookseller. There was a big crowd and it was a happy time. I was so proud of the eight stories in *Unreal* because I had done everything humanly possible to make them attractive to kids, particularly those who didn't like books. I was sure that the stories would hook them in if they gave them a go.

After the speeches we had the usual author book-signing. A small line formed and I dedicated each volume according to the requests of the particular parent or child. Finally, an elderly lady reached the front. 'My grandson John hates books and reading,' she said. 'Write something in the front that will make him read your book.'

I sighed inwardly. Everything I could think of to attract a child had gone into the content. If only you could write a sentence in the front that would guarantee success. I politely scribbled a few words and she departed.

33

Lyndu, who was sixteen at the time, had been watching the signing with great interest. 'That lady didn't look very happy,' she said. 'What did you write?'

I told her.

Dear John,

When you have finished reading this book,

Grandma will give you fifty dollars.

If only it were that simple. Basically, you can't bribe children to like books.

A book for every child

There isn't enough money in the world to lure a child who hates reading into putting in an effort if the material is no good. You need a top story. You need a subject that interests the child. And you need something that they *can* read.

Finding the right book is critical. Believe me, there *is* something that will interest them. Many parents despair because their son or daughter rejects everything they offer. Somewhere along the line the child may have had hurtful experiences with reading. It is intelligent behaviour to avoid pain and seek pleasure. As far as kids' books are concerned, what they want is what they need.

34

I have had countless letters from parents who have told me, 'My son would not look at a book for years. Then suddenly he discovered *Unreal*. Now he won't stop reading.'

It is not always my books they mention. Once at a booksigning a mother rushed to be first in line. 'I just had to tell you how much Peter loves your books. He has read every one. I couldn't get him to read a thing. Then he discovered *Bumface* and that was it.'

I smiled and she left. A little later she came back with a very red face. 'That was Morris Gleitzman's book, wasn't it?' she said quietly. 'I really stuffed up, didn't I?'

She didn't stuff up. She had found the right book for the right child.

Non-fiction

One of my children learned to read from recipe books. He loved cooking, so we bought him a children's cookbook and let him loose in the kitchen. He was incredibly motivated to read difficult words like 'margarine' because he needed them to finish making his cakes. He learned very difficult words quickly because he was keen. Now that he is grown up and can read well, he loves novels. Reading fiction is one of the great pleasures of his life.

GREAT INFORMATION BOOKS

Pre-school
Dig Dig Digging
Margaret Mayo, Alex Ayliffe (illus.)

Infant
Rain
Manya Stojic

Primary
Surprising Shark
Nicola Davies

Horrible Histories series
Terry Deary

Primary and Secondary
Guinness World Records 2003

DK Eyewitness Guides
Subjects ranging from dinosaurs to space exploration

I prefer storybooks for children because they teach us about human behaviour and our place in the world. But I will use anything to get a child reading. I once taught a child to read using the *Sporting Globe* because he loved horse-racing.

Let's face it, many children, especially boys, prefer non-fiction. Racing cars, computers, horses, football, cooking, outer space, animals and fishing are just some of the topics available in information books. True stories like Anne Frank's *The Diary of a Young Girl* can be incredibly interesting and inspiring. These days there are books at various difficulty levels on almost every topic.

Providing that the content is appropriate there is absolutely nothing wrong with comics. They do not establish bad habits. The fact that the pictures make for easy reading is a plus, not a minus. I loved comics as a kid.

36

Wild women

By the time my granddaughter Sarah was five years old, it was obvious that she had an incredibly strong personality. She knew what she wanted even at this young age. She is interested in stories about strong women. She can't tell you why, but she keeps coming back to books like *The Paper Bag Princess* by Robert Munsch, illustrated by Michael Martchenko. This story is about a young woman who does not need to be saved by a chauvinistic prince. She ends up saving *him*. Another favourite of this little girl is *The Twelve Dancing Princesses*. This is a Grimms' fairy tale about wild women who party in the middle of the night against the wishes of their father, the king.

Keep in mind your children's personality characteristics when you select books for them.

Fads – new and old

Don't worry if children's choices seem narrow or unvaried. The main thing is to get them reading and loving it. They will move on. I read every one of W.E. Johns' *Biggles* books when I was thirteen. But I gave them up forty-five years ago. Others have loved Enid Blyton's *Noddy* series or *The Magic Faraway Tree* books for little

37

ones. Don't worry about literary awards. Often the most popular titles miss out. Your children are the best critics when it comes to what they like.

If everyone else is into dinosaurs, or some particular author like J.K. Rowling, feel free to follow the trend with your own child. A few years ago *Goosebumps* books were all the go. These easy-to-read, spooky stories were published at a great rate and anyone who didn't collect them felt left out. If the particular fad is not your cup of tea, you can always introduce your own gems as well. Get a mix. If the latest fashion is poor writing, it will not last. But just because it is popular does not necessarily mean it is not of value.

If your children can't read the books that are popular at school because they find these books too difficult, they *will* feel left out. You can make sure this doesn't happen by reading the popular titles aloud at home. This keeps struggling readers in the picture. Parents wanting to instil a love of reading can use this peer pressure to advantage. There are fashions in books and authors just as there are fashions in dress or games.

You can always sneak in your own favourites but just make sure they are really top stories and not simply a bit of parental nostalgia. Like most parents, I wanted my children to enjoy the books I liked as a child. Sometimes they did, but more often they weren't interested.

By all means, apply your own moral values when you choose books. This is your right, and an issue I discuss in the final chapter. But try not to take an elitist position that denies your children the popular titles.

An easy book can be wonderful

Some parents worry that early books which the children can read by themselves are not good enough or interesting enough when compared to the wonderful classics which are read to them. There is some truth in this, particularly with graded school 'readers', which can be mediocre. But an easy-to-read book can be a wonderful book. When I was a speech therapist I used the *Berenstain Bears* books by Stan and Jan Berenstain with much success. Kids loved the quirky idea of the child being smarter than the silly father.

There are many rhyming books which are easy to read. *Horton Hatches the Egg* by Dr Seuss is a classic which has stood the test of time. The kids in my grade-two class used to love this one.

Start with what the kids are interested in. Then find something that is easy to read. The basic task is to match the interests of the child with the difficulty level of the book. Not easy, but possible. You will find a list of books,

GREAT RHYMING BOOKS

Pre-school

Prowlpuss
Gina Wilson, David Parkins (illus.)

Shark in the Park
Nick Sharratt

Mr McGee
Pamela Allen

Infant

Duck in the Truck
Jez Alborough

Giraffes Can't Dance
Giles Andreae & Guy Parker-Rees

See also p. 67

complete with descriptions, in Chapter 13. This might be a useful starting point.

A young father once approached me and asked me to teach him to read. He was a successful businessman who worked for a petrol company. It was his job to take the monthly records from service stations and recommend sales strategies. Every month, he would take the records home and his wife would read them out to him. Then he would dictate his recommendations. No one at work knew that he couldn't read. When he attended sales conferences he would put his arm in a sling so that he didn't have to write. Or go to the toilet when the questionnaires were handed out.

I asked what had made him finally come for help.

'The other day I left my car parked in the street,' he said. 'When I went to leave I found that someone had parked up close behind my rear bumper. I couldn't get out and I had an urgent appointment to get to. Finally, after an hour or so, the car in front moved and I was able to jiggle my way out. I was absolutely furious and

THIS WEEK WE'LL DO
THE FOUR-LETTER WORDS
THEN NEXT WEEK WE'LL,
WORK UP TO 'BASTARD',
'SCUMBAG' AND 'LOW-LIFE
EXCREMENT MUNCHER'.

wanted to leave a note on the windscreen of the car behind. But I didn't – because I couldn't spell *bastard*.'

He had tears in his eyes when he told me this story. He had waited years before seeking help. The fear of reading can reach phobic proportions. Early failure can stay with a person for their whole life. Not being able to read is a misery. The pain of it quickly leads to avoidance behaviour, and children will develop emotional responses like this man if we give them tasks that are too hard.

So choose carefully, and don't pick books that are too difficult for your children. Every unpleasant experience is a step on the road to reading failure.

41

Difficulty levels

How can you judge the reading level of a book? It takes practice but you will soon gain an intuition about a book's suitability for a particular child. Skim-read the book and make a judgement about the concepts involved in the text. Even if a child can pronounce every word in a book it does not mean they understand it. Reading without meaning is not reading.

Reading is something a person does inside their head. When I was an adult-literacy teacher I once worked with a man who could read a complex sentence like 'I satisfied all the requirements,' but could not match a picture of an apple with the word *apple*.

Pronouncing a word is not reading a word. So make sure that the ideas in a book are not too hard.

The size of words is a rough guide to the difficulty level of a passage. If there are lots of long words, the text is likely to be difficult. This is not an absolute rule, as a word like *lipstick* is easier to read than *cell*, where the *c* makes an unexpected *s* sound.

A more reliable indication of difficulty is sentence length. Children who are struggling will find long sentences with imbedded phrases or clauses difficult to process.

Consider the following sentence, for example.

Alfred, the boy who was carrying the sword, turned
and, remembering what the wizard had taught him
earlier that day, slashed upwards with the blade
and neatly cut off the dragon's head.

'Alfred cut off the dragon's head' is the main bit of this
sentence. But a child who struggles will lose the gist of
this very long sentence before getting there.

I would probably rewrite this passage as:

Alfred fled from the dragon. He remembered what the
wizard had taught him. He turned and slashed upwards
with his sword. The dragon's head fell to the ground.

These smaller chunks are easier to digest because the
ideas are taken in small bites.

ERNEST, IT'S BEAUTIFUL!
I'VE NEVER BEEN SO MOVED
BY A GRADE-TWO
READER.

Nobel-Prize-winners Ernest Hemingway and Samuel Beckett used clear, polished sentences. Simple, clear prose can be more difficult to write than wordy, complex paragraphs which leave the reader bewildered.

Having said this, I don't believe that you can tie the hands of a writer by stopping him or her from using long words or sentences altogether. A good writer for children knows how to balance a story with some long words and some long sentences. It is part of the writer's craft to get it right.

Difficult words can be set up. Take this sentence:

The man was in his cell.

The last word is the most difficult both phonically and conceptually. In this case we can make things easier by making the sentence longer. All we have to do is add one word:

The man was **locked** in his cell.

Now the child has a much better chance of working out *cell* because the word *locked* gives us a clue. I might have considered changing a word:

The **convict** was locked in his cell.

44

Is it easier when we add *convict* or more difficult? I probably wouldn't use this word because the hard *c* in *convict* might make it more likely the child would read *kell* for *cell*. I also considered the words *thief* and *prisoner* as alternatives but they are both complex (*thief* has two consonants making one sound (*th*), and two vowels making another (*ie*); *prisoner* is pronounced *prizoner*).

The look of a book

There are also psychological and social factors to consider in the choice of books. Your selection should not appear too hard to read. Nor should it look too easy. If it seems too difficult, the children won't try. And if it looks babyish, they will be humiliated when their peers see it. We need to find easy-to-read, sophisticated-looking books that won't insult the children. In addition, we have to find something interesting and magical. Something that moves the emotions and causes curiosity, laughter, tears, thrills, anger or anticipation. An un-put-downable book full of joy and wonder.

The look of a book is incredibly important to a child. When my first book was published I requested that it be published as a small paperback with small print and not much white space on the page. That was the fashion at

45

the time in adult books. A lot of white space signalled 'babyish' to the older children – as did illustrations and big print. I was desperate to have a book which a twelve-year-old would be proud to be seen with.

Fashions have changed. Adults now prefer larger books with bigger type and more white space on the page. This is a bit of a relief because these books are much less tiring to read in bed at night. Kids' books have followed the fashion. Publishers can produce junior novels with bigger print and more white space and know that the young reader will not feel humiliated.

In the end, however, it is what is between the covers that counts. And you are able to make a judgement on this. If the parents don't like the book there is a good chance the child won't either. Most children's authors know that a good story will hook in adults too.

This is one of the reasons the *Harry Potter* books by J.K. Rowling are so popular. Adults enjoy reading them. *Harry Potter and the Philosopher's Stone* was possibly the most popular book on the beach the summer after it was released.

It is essential to find a riveting tale – long or short, funny or sad, spooky or whimsical, weird or wondrous. I am always terrified of publishing a story that doesn't grab the reader. The biggest sin in writing is to be boring.

Where are the brilliant books?

46

FRANKLY I FOUND THE ENDING WEAK

You are unlikely to find them in a shelf full of graded series with numbers and colours on their spines. Those texts are editorially controlled for text complexity. There are some gems amongst them but usually the stories are very ordinary. These series may contain books at the appropriate reading levels but you will be very lucky to find a compelling and original tale.

Many schools and educational bookshops contain horrors called 'remedial readers'. These are aimed at the 'reluctant readers' or children who are experiencing difficulty learning to read.

There is no such thing as a book for reluctant readers. If a story does not interest the good readers it will never attract the children who are having difficulties. Writing a book for reluctant readers is like writing a book for people with blue eyes. Reluctant readers have exactly the same needs as other students. They are entitled to a top tale and accessible prose.

47

GREAT READS FOR STRUGGLING READERS

Infant

The Smartest Giant in Town
Julia Donaldson and
Axel Scheffler

Captain Pepper's Pets
Sally Grindley and
David Parkins

Old Tom series
Leigh Hobbs

*Clever Trevor's
Stupendous Inventions*
Andrew Weldon

Flat Stanley
Jeff Brown, Tomi Ungerer
(illus.)

Primary

*The Man Who Wore All His
Clothes*
Allan Ahlberg, Katharine
McEwan (illus.)

Toad Heaven
Morris Gleitzman

The Diary of a Killer Cat
Anne Fine

Secondary

The Fall of Fergal
Philip Ardagh

Frindle
Andrew Clements

Pirate Diary
Richard Platt, Chris Riddell
(illus.)

**Books published by
Barrington Stoke**

It was when I finally realised that it was possible to write easy-to-read prose combined with a top story that my own books took off. I decided to write a book of short stories with interesting and compelling plots. I deliberately made the stories easy to read but I aimed for the good readers as well. Reluctant readers love being able to read what everyone else is reading. I try to attract all the kids with the strength of the plot and the emotional pull. I open the door to the reluctant readers by making the prose accessible. The authors listed on this page do the same.

If your children are bored with their 'readers', I suggest that you approach the teacher and politely ask for something more interesting. Matching children and books is covered in every teacher-training course. It is your right as a parent and the

48

MATCHING KIDS AND BOOKS

FWEEP / TOOT / WAHRP

THE DAY MY BUM WENT PSYCHO
Andy Griffiths

TA DA!

IF I RAN THE CIRCUS
Dr. Seuss

MOTHER, I FIND THESE VOLUMES YOU ARE PROVIDING ME INSUFFICIENTLY CHALLENGING TO MY INTELLECT.

GENERAL THEORY OF RELATIVITY
Albert Einstein

child's right as a student to be given an interesting book at the appropriate level of difficulty.

Books from the heart

Insist on proper books which come from the heart of an author who is compelled to write by the need to tell a story. Don't be fobbed off with educational material which has been written simply to keep the vocabulary at an easy level. Go for a lovely book like *The Neverending Story* by Michael Ende, suitable for ages nine and up.

49

Your local library will have heaps of books and your children's librarian will be happy to help. Don't be afraid to ask. That's what librarians are paid for. Publishers' and authors' websites can also be useful.

A librarian in a school recently told me that she had been renamed as an 'information technologist' so that the school could attract funds for computers. My god, what are we doing? Parents, teachers and librarians can teach the love of books. A computer lacks the human element. We will always need librarians. Kick up a fuss if your library is underfunded, or has an information technologist but no one who loves books.

If you can afford new books, speak to your local booksellers – they nearly always love to give advice. If one doesn't – go to another shop. Or consider searching out specialist children's bookshops.

I used to occasionally give my children the treat of choosing their own titles. Give them a price limit and let them range in the children's section of the shop. If the book is too hard, you can always read it to them.

4

The Importance of Stories

Joining the human race

IN THIS CHAPTER

* Stories help make us honourable members of the human family and tell us that dreams can come true.
* Good stories help us become good people.
* There are two creators of a story – the writer and the reader.
* You can't push a boatload of refugees out into the sea to drown if you survived the terrors of the unforgiving ocean as a fellow traveller – in a book.
* We don't have much to fear from people who have read moving, sensitive stories.
* There are many acts of love that turn children into caring adults. Reading them stories is one of them.

A live crab in a little salty pool on a summer's day. My then five-year-old son was having so much fun that I didn't really mind the effort I had put into finding it for him. And it was a great learning experience. He had already discovered that crabs have claws and will give you a little nip if you aren't careful.

An idyllic scene. A heavenly day. Until the sound of thumping feet approached. I watched two boys about twelve years old running along the sand with boogie boards under their arms. They were scuffling and trying to trip each other as they ran. Showing off and vying for attention. Suddenly they stopped and looked into my son's small pool.

'Look at that,' the biggest boy shouted. 'A bloody crab.' He shoved my son aside and deliberately stamped on the tiny crustacean, killing it instantly. My son began to howl with disappointment and grief at the loss of his little friend, whom he had just named Shelley.

I sprang to my feet. 'Hey, come here, you little . . .'

53

The unfinished sentence hung in the air as the two boys raced away. In a flash they were into the nearby estuary, paddling their boogie boards towards the other side for all they were worth.

'Little gangsters,' I muttered to myself as I picked up my sobbing son and tried to comfort him. 'If I ever get my hands on them I'll . . .' I didn't finish this sentence either. Even if I had caught up with them there was not much I could do. You can't take other people's children to task.

Incidents like these and worse happen every day, everywhere. All over the world there are thoughtless or cruel people who do not know or care what effects their actions have on others.

Tough boys cry too

A couple of months after this incident I was in a school, reading one of my stories to a grade-six class. The story was called 'The Busker', from my book *Unbelievable*. It is about a little dog that dies. Most of my tales are funny but I always include a few more serious stories in my collections. I know it is a moving story because I've had many letters about it from parents and children.

I had almost finished the reading when I looked down at the class to find a boy in the front desk crying over

54

the fate of the little dog and its owner. I was touched to see the way the story had moved him. I was also surprised.

The crying child was the same boy who had jumped on the crab.

This incident had an enormous impact on me. It really drove home how incredibly powerful stories are. They can change people's lives and attitudes. They make us more human. Stories can end suffering and prevent violence. For a little while we become someone else. We know what it is like to be lost and alone. To be shy or anxious or weak. We know what it feels like to get the sack or be the subject of bullying.

My story did more for the crab-stamping lad than being 'grounded' or having his pocket money confiscated would have. He was learning to empathise. He was getting in touch with other people's stories. This is what makes us truly human.

Magic minds

A written story can take us into the mind of another in a way that films and television cannot. The magic minds of the writer and the reader can create a scene that no screen is able to equal. The written word can move us to tears or laughter in a way that nothing else can. A story in a book can perform the most wondrous of feats. It can take us to the ends of the universe.

A story gives us heroes and heroines to copy. A story sets examples. A story cautions. A story points us to the stars. A story can lift us out of a dark place. Stories make us honourable members of the human family and tell us that dreams can come true.

And they do all this by entertaining us. Not everyone likes a sermon. And it is not necessary for stories to preach. I always say that my stories have ethical values because I am a moral person and not because I want to moralise. All good stories help turn us into good people.

Children who don't like books are deprived of one of our most powerful humanising influences. You can't beat up an old lady on the train if you have been into her life or someone like hers in a story. You can't push a boatload of refugees out into the sea to drown if you survived the terrors of the torture chamber and the unforgiving ocean as a fellow traveller – in a book.

I saw what really happened

Stories were told long before there was writing. The Aboriginal peoples of Australia have an incredibly rich collection of stories which were passed on from generation to generation over thousands of years. The oral tradition of storytelling has been valued by all societies. Even today, many young children love to be told family stories about when they were young. Unfortunately, however, due to the pressures of school, work and the lure of computers and television, the oral tradition of storytelling is not as strong in our culture as it once was. This is one of the reasons why written stories are so important today. They are the next best method of telling a tale.

Can computers tell stories? I remember one of my grandchildren having a nightmare. He dreamed that he had used up his last life and had fallen into a fiery pit where he was eaten by a dragon.

'What do you think is behind it?' I asked his mother.

'Oh, he has a computer game in which he fights various enemies. He has five "lives". When they are used up, his screen persona falls into the pit and is eaten. The screen says BAD LUCK JOHN YOU ARE DEAD.'

No wonder John had a bad nightmare. The computer actually used the child's name to maximise the character identification. If I wrote a story in which the main character fought gory battles one after another, killing or being killed, no one would publish it. The dragon game is not a proper story. It has no moral values and no journey other than a series of battles.

The makers of computer software are slowly becoming aware of this problem. Some of the interactive programs now include moral and ethical values. The character or hero has the chance on a quest to make choices which are brave but also involve self-sacrifice, persistence and humility. Wise and compassionate choices increase the player's chances of winning. These games are available on the Internet and can be played against other competitors far across the world.

They are a type of storytelling. But the participant is a player. They are going on their own journey and not someone else's. Depending on the quality of the experience, these games may be valuable. The difference is subtle, but the computer journey is a game, while the one taken in a book is a story. They are not the same thing.

It can be argued that television and movies tell stories. And tell them well. I can hardly disagree with this as I have written scripts turning my own stories into television series (the first two series of 'Round the Twist'). However, a screen will never be able to replace the amazing scenes which a reader creates in their own mind when they devour a book. There are limitations of budget and scale. Even the 3D IMAX screen cannot produce the scenes imagined by the human mind. At any one moment there are two creators of a story – the writer and the amazing mind of the reader. I recall talking to a mother who thought my story 'A Dozen Bloomin' Roses' was too gory for children. She said, 'I can still see it. The boy was trapped in the tunnel. The train bore down on him. He threw up his handful of flowers in despair and was smashed down in a spray of blood.'

I turned to the page in my story, horrified at her response. I had handled that scene with enormous care so as not to frighten the children who read the story. I read aloud what I had written to the concerned parent:

> The train rushed out of the tunnel. As it slowed
> I noticed a bunch of broken flower stems wedged
> on one of the buffers.

'That's all I wrote,' I protested.

'Yes,' she replied. 'But in my mind I saw what really happened.'

Since that discussion I have made a point never to forget how much of themselves a reader will bring to my stories. Parents should be aware of advanced readers getting their hands on books which they can read but for which they are not emotionally prepared. I try very hard not to frighten children. And I don't present the world as a bleak and horrible place.

Sometimes people do die in my stories. But I always

59

have a happy ending. Most people who know about children's books demand hope as a minimum in tales for primary-school children.

We can go further than hope and also provide joy, courage, wonder, laughter and compassion. A story helps us become members of the community of reasonable people.

This love of stories – this participation in the human drama – starts early. So if we really care for our kids, we will move heaven and earth to get them into books from the very beginning. It is not necessary for me to state how much we love our children. We want to protect them from the smallest unnecessary pain. But we also want them to be sensitive to the pain of others.

No one will play with the little duck

I remember being called to the school of my daughter Lyndu, who was five at the time. 'She is crying so much that we can't get a word out of her,' said the principal's voice on the phone. 'Could you come and see what is going on? We are worried she might have swallowed something.'

I raced to the school. There she was, sobbing and gasping for breath.

'What's up, sweetheart? Tell Daddy.'

Still she couldn't get the words out. I became desperate. 'We'd better take her to hospital.'

'Why not ask her sister?' said a teacher.

Tracy was eighteen months older than Lyndu. Maybe she could shed some light on the problem.

Tracy was brought from her class and left alone to talk with her distraught sister. We all waited anxiously outside the door. Finally, Tracy came out.

'She's crying because no one will play with the little duck.'

Our jaws dropped. Lyndu's teacher had been reading them *The Ugly Duckling*. The play bell had rung before the happy ending where the ugly and rejected duckling grows into a beautiful swan that finds its true family. Lyndu was bereft at the thought of the poor little duck having no one to play with.

Hans Christian Andersen certainly knew how to

GREAT STORIES TO MOVE THE EMOTIONS

Pre-school

Can't You Sleep, Little Bear?
Martin Waddell, Barbara Firth (illus.)

Infant

The Little Match Girl
Hans Christian Andersen

Granpa
John Burningham

Primary

Charlotte's Web
E.B. White, Garth Williams (illus.)

The Owl Tree
Jenny Nimmo, Anthony Lewis (illus.)

Bridge to Terabithia
Katherine Paterson

The Snow Goose
Paul Gallico

Two Weeks with the Queen
Morris Gleitzman

Secondary

To Kill a Mockingbird
Harper Lee

Roll of Thunder, Hear My Cry
Mildred D. Taylor

61

write a good yarn. What a story. A timeless classic that has moved millions of people. A theme that has been told in different forms since our ancestors lived in caves.

Both of these little girls have grown up to be sensitive and caring adults. Both of them have always loved books. We don't have much to fear from people who have read moving, sensitive stories. But the habit starts early. There are many acts of love that turn children into imaginative, caring adults. Reading them stories is one of them.

62

5

Preschool and Beginners

Like the words of a song

IN THIS CHAPTER

* Every child matures at a different rate.
* You can help prepare your child for the early years of school.
* They feel they are reading.
* When to start school.
* Peer pressure.
* Early books of joy and fun.
* Yabber is real reading.

Howls of protest will arise if you try to finish early by skipping a couple of pages in a story. Children want it all done properly. They can't be fooled.

"ONCE UPON A TIME THERE WERE THESE 3 LITTLE PIGS AND UM... THEY HAD SOME ADVENTURES, AND ALL LIVED HAPPILY EVER AFTER THE END"

HEY!!

Like the words of a song

Repeated readings of favourite stories lead to the whole book becoming internalised like the words of a song.

65

This is a very useful phenomenon. The children know the words of the story before they are able to recognise them in print. As they leaf through the book on their own or listen to you read it aloud they begin to recognise individual words. They are on their way.

It can be useful to point to words as you read to children. Don't put pressure on them to read but do occasionally draw attention to the print – particularly key words. Books which only have one or two words on a page are especially valuable.

Sometimes children will learn a whole book by heart. They will 'read' along with you. Don't spoil this by pointing out their mistakes or requiring them to identify words unless they want to. They enjoy joining in and feel that they are 'reading'. Maintain the illusion and it will turn into reality eventually. Rhyming stories, like the ones listed here, help kids to predict what is coming next.

Stories which use a lot of repetition like Dr Seuss's *Green Eggs and I am* enable the child to predict what is coming next. The rhyming word at the end of the next line is usually expected and the preceding words are often repeated. The child reader can easily follow the pattern. (See extract on page 120.)

MORE GREAT RHYMING BOOKS

Each Peach Pear Plum
Allan Ahlberg, Janet Ahlberg (illus.)

The Cat in the Hat
Dr Seuss

I Want to be a Cowgirl
Jeanne Willis and Tony Ross

Various books by Pamela Allen

Various books by Lynley Dodd

Madeline
Ludwig Bemelmans

What on Earth Can It Be?
Roger McGough, Lydia Monks (illus.)

See also p. 40

When to start school

A vexed question at the preschool age is how old a child should be when they start school. Working parents often have a lot of pressure on them with this question.

There is no simple answer because each child is different and matures at a different rate. Some kids walk at ten months and some at eighteen months. Both are within

67

GREAT BOOKS WITHOUT MANY WORDS ON A PAGE

Handa's Surprise
Eileen Browne

Pants
Giles Andreae and Nick Sharratt

Dinosaur Roar!
Paul and Henrietta Stickland

Spot Goes to the Park
Eric Hill

Rosie's Walk
Pat Hutchins

normal limits. Similarly, some children's language skills can be very advanced. Differences in word knowledge and grammar of up to six months can be found in children about to start school.

Let's consider the following case. A five-and-a-half-year-old is six months advanced (performing linguistically like the average six-year-old). Next to him at school is a four-and-a-half-year-old who is six months delayed (performing like the average four-year-old). Although both children are within normal limits there is actually a two-year difference in their linguistic skills.

If the school is understanding and gives both children rewarding learning experiences at the appropriate level, the above scene may not be too worrying. But if the four-year-old perceives that they are failing at early reading tasks a negative attitude may be the catastrophic result. A child's self-perception as an under-achieving reader is the cause of most reading problems.

All things being equal, I would prefer to wait another year before starting the four-year-old described

above at school. I am well aware that this might not be possible for many families. Parents who work or who have other important responsibilities at home are understandably keen to get their children into school. But it is better to start children at school a year later than to make them repeat a year in the future.

I remember one little boy I'll name Craig, who was so far behind at the end of his second year at school that he faced constant failure every day at school. The teachers and children were not cruel to Craig but he was aware that he just couldn't read at all. It embarrassed and humiliated him. His behaviour began to deteriorate.

Craig was good at sport and a leader in the playground. The prospect of 'staying down' appalled him. He refused. He cried. He shouted and swore when the idea was even mentioned. There was no way that he was

going to be seen associating with 'little kids' and lose his status or be ridiculed.

At the end of the school year the whole family moved to a new town. Craig didn't want to move schools but he realised that none of the children in the new school would know he was repeating a year. The parents and teachers promised that it would be kept a secret and he accepted the decision with ease. This incident illustrates the strength of peer pressure.

If you think your children are a little behind in language skills when they are approaching school age, seek the advice of your preschool teacher or a speech therapist.

Be very sensitive to the tasks that are given in the early years of school. When books are sent home with a requirement that the child read aloud, the task must be easily accomplished. Failure and struggle in the early years will lead to avoidance.

70

In order to prepare your child well, it is best to select books which maximise the chance of a predictable pattern being laid down in the child's mind. When we choose these sorts of books the instant recognition of letters and words becomes unnecessary. The sentences in these early books contain nothing but joy and fun. And they are easy to read. I will say more about this in the following chapter.

Listening to children read

When was the last time you read aloud? If you are a teacher, professional speaker or an actor it may have been quite recently. But most people hardly ever read aloud. If you think about it your life is not likely to be ruined if you never read aloud again. It is not a big part of life for most of us. Handy but not essential.

GREAT FIRST BOOKS OF JOY AND FUN

Brown Bear, Brown Bear, What Do You See?
Bill Martin Jnr, Eric Carle (illus.)

Cowboy Baby
Sue Heap

Mr McGee
Pamela Allen

Who Sank the Boat?
Pamela Allen

We're Going on a Bear Hunt
Helen Oxenbury, Michael Rosen (Illus.)

Dogger
Shirley Hughes

Frog Finds a Friend
Max Velthuijs

The Gruffalo
Julia Donaldson and Axel Scheffler

Mister Magnolia
Quentin Blake

Not Now, Bernard
David McKee

Dear Zoo
Rod Campbell

Mr Gumpy's Outing
John Burningham

71

If you can't read silently, however, you are stuffed.

When you look in your child's bedroom and find them so captured by a book that they don't hear the call to dinner you have achieved the ultimate goal. We hope that this child will also be able to read aloud to the class but we are not going to lose too much sleep if they can't. Okay, later it will be a valuable skill to be able to stand up in front of a board of directors or a local conservation group and read out a report. But it won't be nearly as important as being able to read the report to themselves.

Lying on a bed laughing, crying, wondering and wandering in some far-off imaginary world created in your head by a skilled writer is fantastic. Struggling to

figure out unknown words on a page and pronounce them correctly can be agony.

So why do we ask children to read aloud?

Teachers ask parents to listen to children reading aloud in the evenings because it is the main way to measure their progress. It is a diagnostic and learning exercise. Reading aloud is a tool which leads to the ultimate goal of finding a child alone, except for the wonderful characters on the page. Silent reading is not only allowed. It is essential.

Yabber is pure gold

Children can 'read' to themselves from a very early age – maybe as young as two years. You will notice the beginnings of this development with picture books, where the child will simply turn the page looking at the pictures and retelling the story internally. Sometimes they will vocalise under their breath and you will notice that they are using their own words, not the ones on the page. Don't correct them. If you tell them they are wrong, you will spoil their pleasure.

A mother once told me that her daughter turned over the pages and tried to read the words. 'But it was just yabber.'

'No,' I said. 'It is pure gold.' Yabber is an early stage of reading.

We may be tempted to feel that real reading starts with learning the sounds of letters or recognising individual words. Nothing could be further from the truth. The early retelling of a story by a child where they approximate the meaning of the print is real reading. Encourage and reward it.

GREAT BOOKS WHICH ALMOST READ THEMSELVES

Preschool

There's Something at the Letter Box
Jez Alborough

Titch
Pat Hutchins

Hairy Maclary from Donaldson's Dairy
Lynley Dodd

This is the Bear
Sarah Hayes, Helen Craig (illus.)

Eat Your Peas
Kes Gray, Nick Sharratt (illus.)

See also p. 85

The desperate whisper

I recall reading aloud at school when I was a boy in grade five. Every person in the class of fifty-two had the same book. We all opened at the same page for 'reading'. The child in the front desk read the first two sentences aloud and then stopped. The next child took over and so it went, moving along the rows of desks. Mispronouncing or not knowing a word was something to be feared. Depending on the teacher, one could be strapped, admonished or humiliated in some way or other. Kids with reading problems suffered terrible emotional traumas.

Of course, most of us had figured out which sentences we would be required to read aloud when our turn came. 'What's that word?' we would desperately whisper to a friend. The poor kids who couldn't read at all waited like condemned prisoners for their moment of terror. How they longed for lunchtime and freedom. To these children, 'being saved by the bell' had real meaning.

There are still adults who are too shy to read or even speak in public because of the humiliations they suffered when performing in front of a class.

Reading aloud from a book to a loving parent can be fun and free from fear. But it can also be a disagreeable and unpleasant struggle if it isn't done properly. There is no room for impatience. There is no room for failure. There is no room for struggle. Sighs, nervous tics and anxious questions from the children like, 'How long to go?' are sure signs that all is not well.

This unpleasant battle with oral reading can happen at home or school. The consequences of a child failing with reading aloud can last a lifetime. Once a child relates books to pain we have a big problem. Parents must also look as if they are enjoying the experience. Children are very sensitive to non-verbal messages.

Listen carefully

Listening is a skill that most of us have not fully developed. My friend, the writer Ted Greenwood, was the greatest listener I have ever met. People loved him for the way he looked into their eyes and drank in every word. They appreciated his kind queries and comments. No matter who he was speaking to, he concentrated on their thoughts and propositions with loving attention. He never drifted off into his own reverie. He refused to let his eyes glaze over with boredom.

Good therapists teach themselves how to listen. All of us could work at developing listening skills. Especially with our children.

THE WRONG WAY

HONEY, WHY DON'T YOU READ INTO DADDY'S DICTAPHONE AND DADDY WILL LISTEN TO IT ON THE WAY TO WORK TOMORROW.

THE <u>VERY</u> GOOD LISTENER

This is also important when you listen to a child read. They are making an offering of love. They are telling you a story. If you are not interested and caring, you are rejecting this love. And the rejection of love is one of the most painful experiences we can suffer.

We all close our ears sometimes. Parents are only human. I remember bailing up my long-suffering mother once when she was cooking. I was about eleven and had just returned from the Melbourne Motor Show with a pile of car pamphlets. I was crazy about cars, and started leafing through each pamphlet, telling her the specifications and excitedly proclaiming the features of the various vehicles. A bit later my father said she had asked him to instruct me not to bother her when she was so busy. I was terribly hurt. All these years later I still remember the rejection.

Of course, my mother hadn't done anything wrong.

We can't stand around listening to everything children want to say or we would never get anything done. But they do perceive our boredom or lack of interest and it is a form of punishment. Perhaps she could have asked me to tell her about the car leaflets later. It would have been a wonderful opportunity for purpose-related, fun reading. Car pamphlets, horse books and toy catalogues will sometimes be avidly devoured when almost every other form of reading is rejected.

So don't listen to the children's oral reading while you are washing up or watching the news on television. Set yourself up for a bit of fun with your child. Get a quiet place, warm and safe. And then go for it.

78

6

Reading for Meaning

It's okay to speed ahead

IN THIS CHAPTER

* Smoothing the path for reading success.
* A few simple ways to use context.
* The book literally reads itself.
* Good writing is almost invisible.
* Meaning is our greatest clue.
* It is okay to speed ahead and get the odd word wrong.
* Discovery learning lasts a lifetime.
* Listening to a rascal.

I had failed and I didn't like it. Forty-six years after it happened I can still remember scoring nine marks out of a possible twenty on a comprehension passage at school. My friend Kelvin scored twenty out of twenty. 'Geez,' I said. 'You did well.'

The passage was from an unknown book and it was something to do with people on a boat. I couldn't figure out where they were or what they were doing. It was really frustrating. There just wasn't enough information in the three paragraphs provided to enable me to answer the questions properly. And yet my friend had done it easily.

'I've read the book the passage came out of,' said Kelvin. 'It was called *The Kon-Tiki Expedition.*'

I have to say I was annoyed. That's why I've remembered this incident for all these years. My friend Kelvin had an unfair advantage. He knew that the story written by Thor Heyerdahl was about a raft drifting across the Pacific Ocean. He had recognised the name of one of the characters and the whole thing fell into place.

Keep it in context

The context is incredibly useful information when we read. It helps us predict what is going to happen. It helps us to understand what the main ideas are. And it makes new words and terminology easier to figure out.

When you listen to your son or daughter read at home you can use context to make things easier for them. There are a few simple ways in which you can use context.

How about letting the child read from a book that you have already read to them? Okay, so they already know the story and the enjoyment may be lessened. But all kids have their favourites and sometimes the pleasure is increased by subsequent readings. And anyway, success in reading a story that you have heard before is preferable to failure with a new one.

If you pick a favourite story such as *The Three Billy Goats Gruff*, even if it is a different version, the children will know what to expect. It will be much easier for them to figure out the unknown words. The billy goats, the bridge and the troll will all be anticipated. The kids will be able to rock and roll with this story without a single 'lesson'. They will have lots of fun.

One of the great benefits of nursery rhymes is the way they quickly become implanted in the memory.

Once we hear 'Humpty Dumpty sat on a wall', we are able to provide the next line. This is real reading. It is not cheating or too easy but a legitimate way of easing the path. The book literally reads itself.

Another example of this smoothing of the path is found in *There's Something at the Letter Box*, a peep-through book by Jez Alborough*. A similar format, and mostly the same words, are found on each page. A big eye peeps through the letter box on the right-hand page.

> 'Dad, there's something at the letter box. What can it be?'
> **'Be brave, Billy boy, have a look and see.'**

We turn the page to see that the eye belongs to a crocodile.

> 'Dad, it's a **crocodile**. What shall I do?'
> **'Ask it in, Billy boy, it can play with you.'**

The same pattern is repeated with a tiger and a bear. On the last page it is Dad who is peeping – he is dressed up as Tarzan. This funny story uses rhyming, picture clues

* Extract taken from *There's Something at the Letter Box* © 1995 Jez Alborough. Reproduced by permission of Walker Books Ltd., London.

and repetition to ensure that after one or two exposures almost any child can read it alone.

Before I ask a child to read a new story to me I will often read the first couple of pages aloud to him or her. This has incredible value. For one thing it sets up some of the hard words and the names of the characters.

People's names like *Philippa*, *Siobhan* and *Mr Billingheimer* are difficult to read. So are place names like *Australia*, *Warrnambool* and *Brighton*. If the child has heard you pronounce them, they will not have to struggle when they come across these words themselves. With this strategy you don't have to spoil the enjoyment by turning the reading time into a lesson. You have 'taught' these names simply by reading the first few pages.

A variation on this theme is to take turns and read alternate pages. You first and then the child.

Another good idea is to choose books about a well-loved topic. A child who is mad about motorbike racing will know terms and concepts like *carburettor* and *cylinder head*. Someone else who is crazy about horses will know *palomino* and *fetlock*.

When a child struggles with an individual word and is left for many seconds trying to make sense of it they may lose track of the meaning of the passage. Words in a story are like links on a bicycle chain. If words are treated as separate entities, the intangible joy and purpose of the story is lost. The bicycle doesn't go any more. Links in a chain are not particularly interesting or useful on their own. And while words may retain meaning on their own they have a lot more when they are part of a whole. A story is a journey. It starts somewhere and it goes somewhere. It is interesting. It is funny or scary or weird or sad. Children will lose all the fun if they spend too long trying to decode individual words. A hiker who has to stop and concentrate on every sixth or seventh step will soon give up bushwalking.

> **MORE GREAT BOOKS WHICH ALMOST READ THEMSELVES**
>
> **Babies**
>
> *The Dorling Kindersley Book of Nursery Rhymes*
> Debi Gliori
>
> *Skip Across the Ocean, Nursery Rhymes from Around the World*
> Ed. Floella Benjamin, Sheila Moxley (illus.)
>
> *Brown Bear, Brown Bear, What Do You See?*
> Bill Martin Jnr, Eric Carle (illus.)
>
> *Ginger*
> Charlotte Voake
>
> See also p. 74

Reading for general meaning rather than total accuracy results in more pleasure being gained from the reading experience. But the notion is controversial.

Kids don't build Boeing jets

I remember one objection from a colleague. I was working in my office at the university when an irate science lecturer burst in and plonked himself on a chair. I was in charge of a subject called Language Curriculum. It involved training student teachers in the instruction of reading, spelling and oral language in primary schools.

'Paul,' he growled. 'The Teacher Education students tell me you have been suggesting that it is okay for children to guess words when they read aloud.'

'That's a simplification,' I said. 'But basically, yes.'

'And if it's a word with a similar meaning you just let the mistake go?'

'Yes.'

'That's crazy,' he yelped. 'What if they are designing a bridge or assembling a Boeing jet or writing a prescription for a patient? Near enough is not good enough. People could die.'

'But children don't design bridges or assemble jets or write prescriptions.'

'They will one day. You're telling teachers to start bad habits in kids that will last for a lifetime. It's disgraceful. Once the guessing habit is formed they will never get out of it.'

'But reading for accuracy is a higher order skill. We can teach it later. In the early stages the kids need to read for the general meaning and enjoyment, not word-for-word accuracy.'

The argument went on for an hour or so and finally he went off promising to raise the matter at our faculty board. He was sure the mathematics department would support his objections.

As you can guess, this issue is a hot potato in some circles. Most teachers these days, however, realise that there are sound arguments for allowing children to get the gist of a passage without interrupting them every time they make a 'mistake'.

Reading for meaning rather than word-for-word accuracy is not my idea. I wish it was. But a number of people, including the brilliant linguists Frank Smith and Ken Goodman, developed this notion in the early 1970s. At the time, unfortunately, many teachers including myself made the poor kids stop at every word they didn't know when they were reading aloud. It took us some time to catch up and realise just how frustrating and counterproductive it was.

So what are the issues?

Well, let's first admit that there are different types of reading. When you are tuning in a channel on your video player you are a lot more careful with reading the individual words in the instruction book than you are when racing through a Mills and Boon romance. Adult readers skip words, paragraphs and even pages. Imagine how annoying and time consuming it would be if you were required to take in every word when you read a novel.

87

ANY WORD IN THE RECIPE I COULDN'T UNDERSTAND I JUST SKIPPED OVER.

I make it a rule with my books that I will not ask children to do any reading task that adults don't do. Sometimes I get a request for a story to be published with a set of comprehension questions at the end. I always say no. Good grief. Who cares what colour shoes the girl was wearing or how many times the boy scratched himself? Questions at the end take all the joy out of racing through a story to see what happens next.

It is okay to speed ahead and get the odd word wrong. Adults do it all the time.

And of course it is possible to know roughly what a word means without being able to pronounce it. I knew that the *Sigh-Uks* were a tribe of Indians long before I realised that *Sioux* was pronounced *Sue. Horse doovers* is another famous example. Like many others, for years I didn't realise *hors d'oeuvres* was pronounced *orderve*. The main thing is to know the meaning. In the end someone will help with your pronunciation.

Meaning is our greatest clue

Is it really a 'mistake' when a child substitutes a word with a similar meaning to one in the story?

Consider this sentence:

The boy climbed the _____ and grabbed some _____ .

What is the first missing word? It could be anything – *ladder, wall, monument, rock* – it is impossible to say what the boy climbed. If I tell you that the second missing word is *leaves*, you will probably come up with *tree* for the first missing word. If I tell you that the first letter of the first word is *b*, you may guess that he climbed a *branch*. But the missing word is really *birch*.

Birch is a hard word to read, and a child may make the 'mistake' of saying *branch* when he or she is reading to you. In a story about a magical burglar, does it really matter if he climbed a *birch* or a *branch*? It is better to let the child read on. He or she has made an approximation based on meaning and has probably used the first letter *b* as a clue. *Branch* is a good 'guess'. The child is reading for meaning.

If you make the children stop and sound the whole word out, they will have to know that *ir* says *er* (but not in *biro*) and that *ch* says *tch* (but not in *machine*).

89

Having to stop and sound out words is frustrating. It is unpleasant. It is often impossible.

Letting the child use the context to have a stab at the meaning in this case is more useful than sounding out the letters. The guessed word, *branch*, is a sensible approximation. Sounding out each letter in *birch* will probably lead to the creation of a nonsense word such as *b-i-rr-i-ck-huh*.

The very word 'mistake' is misleading. The linguist Kenneth Goodman came up with the term 'miscues' for the child's attempts to work out what a word is. He wanted us to see these 'errors' as useful indications of the strategies that children are using. Parents don't have to worry about Goodman's technique of miscue analysis, which is a method of observing the cues that children use to make sense of an unknown word. The general principles, however, are easy to apply. Here is an example which illustrates a way of interpreting an 'incorrect' response.

Take this sentence:

'I use soap to *wash* my face.'

A child who reads, 'I use soap to *watch* my face,' is not reading for meaning. His miscue tells us this fact. He or she is using a sound clue to figure out the unknown word. Another child may read, 'I use soap to *clean* my face,' which is a better response.

The second child's response is better because they have guessed based on meaning (*clean* instead of *wash*). The first child has guessed based on the sound of the word (*watch* instead of *wash*) and has come up with a nonsense sentence. With the first child we could say, 'Does that make sense?' Of the second child we might ask, 'Does *clean* start with *w*?' I would prefer, however, to let the second child's response go unremarked. We may choose to ignore the 'mistake' of *clean* for *wash* because the child is reading for meaning and we don't want to interrupt the flow and spoil the moment. Too many interruptions turn the whole exercise into torture.

Meaning is our greatest clue when figuring out unknown words. If you tell children not to guess, you

91

deprive them of the technique that you yourself use most often when you read.

Camels can fly

When I am writing a story I often 'set up' a difficult word so that the child has the maximum chance of guessing it or at least knowing what the meaning might be. Consider this passage from my book *Tongue-Tied*. It concerns a boy who can see his dead brother through a pair of marvellous glasses. His brother cannot see him. Suddenly he is inspired.

> *Plop.* Yes, the lens flipped out. Then the other one. *Plop.* The wire frame was empty. I had done it. I stared at the two glass lenses. Then I quickly threw one of them into the box. It shimmered and vanished.
>
> I pushed the remaining lens on to one eye and closed the other. It was a lens for one eye. A monocle.
>
> It worked. I could see Gavin through my left eye. He was putting his lens up to his right eye. He could see me.
>
> 'G'day,' he said in a cheeky voice.

When I wrote that passage I worked hard to set up the word *monocle*, which would be unfamiliar to most young children. It is defined quite clearly by the preceding sentences. Notice also the short paragraphs which are easy to decode. The passage also demonstrates another of my rules. I always use a new paragraph for each piece of dialogue. It is very important that the children know which character is speaking.

I have been criticised for using techniques such as this which make my books easy to read. Some say it is 'not proper literature' if you modify the text to make it accessible. What a lot of nonsense. I have a heap of strategies and I employ them deliberately. Children are learning to read. You don't offer a newborn baby roast beef and you don't offer the average ten-year-old a book by Tolstoy. And anyway, good writing does not have to be full of similes, metaphors and adjectives. Ernest Hemingway knew this. Try *The Old Man and the Sea* if you want wonderful, spare prose for older readers.

In my book *Unmentionable* I wrote a story called 'Little Squirt'. It was a funny tale about a small boy who couldn't pee as high as his older brother. The writing was easy to read. In the same book was another story called 'The Mouth Organ' which I wrote in complex, poetic language. The book was reviewed in a prestigious magazine. The article quoted a passage of mine from

'The Mouth Organ' which metaphorically calls up the effect of the magical mouth organ music on the listeners.

I usually avoid metaphors because children find them difficult to understand. For example, the metaphor, 'the cold hand of fate grabbed me by the throat', will often leave a child wondering where the cold hand came from. For some reason I let myself go in the story about the mouth organ. I regret it now. When I wrote 'The Mouth Organ' I forgot about my readers and indulged myself.

The reviewer loved the story and quoted the following passage.

> I take them sailing on sparkling oceans. I fly them through the clouds. I show them the bottom of the sea and the highest mountain peaks. Places where the air is so crisp it tinkles when you breathe. I shower them in a waterfall. I dust them with moon powder. I rock them in the arms of loved ones long passed on.
>
> It is the sound of the birth of the world. It is a flower opening. It is a mother's tear plopping on her baby's cheek. It is a foal's first steps. It is the promise of new life.

I felt guilty for years for using so much metaphor and simile in that story. But the reviewer loved it and went

94

on to say, 'This from a writer who in the preceding story has the triumphant little boy claim, "Boy, do I squirt. I pee higher than anyone in the world has ever done." Confused? I have a feeling that Paul Jennings is too.'

I think I *was* confused, but not in the way the reviewer thought. I allowed myself, I think for the first and only time, to please the adults instead of the children. The piece which I now least value was most liked by the reviewer. It is amazing and distressing to see how easily we can force our own preferences on children.

I wrote the story 'Little Squirt' into a script which went on to be made into an episode of 'Round the Twist'. It won the coveted international Prix Jeunesse Award for excellence in children's television. I have had hundreds of letters from children about this story. Without a doubt it is my most popular piece of writing.

I have not received one letter about 'The Mouth Organ'.

Idiom can cause problems for adults too. I remember being at a dinner party where two teenage girls dropped their jaws in silent shock at one of their mother's comments. They then broke into uncontrolled laughter. The poor lady had simply said, 'Sometimes I feel like a shag on a rock.'

The girls did not know that piece of idiom. To them a 'shag' was not a bird but something different altogether.

We adults often prefer the intricate to the intelligible, and the complex to the concrete. Good writing is

95

not inaccessible. It does not draw attention to itself. It is almost invisible as it leads the child into the story.

Children *want* to know what the story is about. They will fight for meaning if they are allowed. I remember reading a Biggles book when I was about eleven. The hero had gone from Alexandria to Cairo by Camel. The journey took an hour. I recall thinking to myself, 'Geez, that must have been a fast camel.' It annoyed me. I knew that such a trip was impossible. This wasn't a fantasy book. Peter Pan might have been able to do the trip but not Biggles who, if you look closely, *was* a Peter Pan of types. He flew around the world, didn't drink, didn't age and had no time for women. But he was presented as a real person and not a magician. He couldn't have done the trip in an hour.

Finally I noticed the capital *C*. The Camel was a First World War aeroplane.

Encourage meaning as a clue. You will find that the question, 'Does that make sense?' is often more useful than the command, 'Sound that out.'

If the child is missing the meaning of the story altogether, then the book is too hard. If the unknown words are so frequent that they cause frustration, the same thing applies. Don't persist. Find another book.

Remember, the first aim is to have fun. The second is to get meaning from print. Forget this and you end up with hokey-pokey. And that's *not* what it's all about.

96

Guessing is good

I suggested earlier that guessing can be good. But the children are not really 'guessing' at all. If a word giving difficulty is incorrectly read as a different word with similar meaning it is not usually a guess. We are tempted to think that they pick a word from nowhere. But more often they will make a deduction rather than a guess. Consider this sentence:

The monkey climbed up the *waterfall*.

What could that last word be? Your son or daughter doesn't know. They are unlikely to guess as follows:

The monkey climbed up the *was*.

That sentence just isn't right. By a miraculous process which we still do not fully understand, children know all about the correct order of the various parts of speech in a sentence. They have never heard of nouns, verbs, adjectives and articles but they instinctively know what follows what. They learn the rules for ordering the words without one lesson. They know that *was* is not likely to follow *the*.

They also know that the sentence doesn't make sense. You are much more likely to get an 'error' of *wall*

97

substituted for *waterfall* because it is a possible (and more likely) alternative. In this case the child has also chosen a word that starts with the same letter.

Usually, the child is not guessing when they read a word incorrectly. They are using a large number of clues to figure out the most likely alternative. They are making approximations. The child who read *was* for *waterfall* was using the strategy of the sound of the first letter but was not making use either of meaning or grammatical cues.

This is useful information for the adult who is listening. This child was not reading for meaning. So they were not reading at all. Reading is not pronouncing words. I could probably pronounce most words in an instruction book for servicing a phantom jet. But I wouldn't have the faintest idea what it was all about.

No matter what the age – if your child is not understanding what they are reading, they are not reading. So abandon ship. Find something that they can understand and start with easier or more interesting material.

There are simple techniques to use which can make an incredible difference when you listen to a child read. On the surface, these are simple and easy strategies which are second nature to most teachers. Simple they may be, but they embody profound truths and are based on experience and research that has been undertaken by many thousands of people all over the world.

Difficult words

Most of the difficulties parents have when they listen to reading relates to difficult words. How you respond is very important. Here's an example.

Let's take a word that I used in Chapter 4.

Crustacean. A boy called Stefan is trying to read the following sentence but is stumped by the hard word:

The old man was trying to catch the *crustacean.*

There may be a picture on the opposite page. The illustration could be of a man trying to catch a crab in a pool at the beach. Stefan may respond with *crab* because the word *crustacean* begins with the letters *cr.* He has 'guessed' based on the first letter in the word. That's what the teacher may have been telling him to do. 'Sound it out.' Or he may have been instinctively using his knowledge of the sounds of words. But he can't sound out the rest of the word because the last bit is too hard (particularly the second *c* which says *sh*).

Stefan made a good response and used the meaning of the sentence, the picture and the first sounds in the word to figure it out. His miscue is not a guess but, in the strictest sense, it is incorrect.

How should the parent respond?

Here are a number of possible responses. All of them are correct in some situations. It is a matter of balancing the various factors. The most important concern is the enjoyment of the child. Any strategy that leads to suffering is the wrong strategy.

1 Ignore the mistake

We must remember that it is not a mistake but a miscue. *Crab* was a good attempt based on meaning. *Crab* makes sense. If I had been writing the story, I would have written *crab* and not *crustacean* for younger readers. The child has lost very little meaning if you allow this approximation to pass.

If the word comes up over and over again, you may

wish to point out what the word really is. Your decision will be based on balance. How many times have you corrected the child? It is unpleasant to be corrected. So let a few of these sensible substitutions through. If there are too many unknown words the book is too hard.

2 Tell Stefan what the word is as soon as he hesitates

Certainly this is much better than leaving the poor child to struggle over a word which is probably not in his vocabulary and is phonically very complex. The illustration which is aimed at seven-year-olds tells me that the child is too young to be tackling words like this.

3 Suggest that Stefan look at the picture for a clue

Yes, a good strategy. One of the reasons the picture is there is to provide help with identifying the words. Some books put the picture on a different page to the relevant part of the text just to stop the child 'guessing'. Crazy stuff. We need to make the whole experience as easy as possible. When I was a young teacher I was taught to bang my hand down over the picture as soon as the child turned the page. The poor kids were not allowed to see the illustration until they had read the words. Now I let them have a good look at the illustration before they read the words. This is setting them up for success, not failure.

4 Suggest that Stefan skip the word and read on for more information

This is a useful strategy if used with care. Adults do this with unknown words and usually figure out the meaning from the later context. Don't overdo it, and make it fun. The child could read 'blah, blah' for a difficult word and have a shot at it later. The passage may go on as follows:

> The old man was trying to catch the crustacean.
> But he was scared that the crab would bite him.

By reading ahead, the meaning of the unknown word has become clear without us having to 'teach' anything.

5 Glance through the book first and explain any hard words

If you can do this in a fun, non-teacherly manner, it can be useful. Remember that reading time is meant to be fun time. Not unpleasant work.

And remember to pick the right book and set the reading time up so that the child will have a good chance of figuring out most of the difficult words. Turn back to page 53 and my anecdote about the boy who stamped on a crab and you will find that I set up the word *crustacean* for any reader who might not be into aquatic science.

These sorts of strategies mean that Stefan can learn without being taught. Every teacher knows that discovery learning lasts a lifetime. Lessons often drop from memory like leaves tumbling in autumn.

Rascal the Dragon

Here is the draft for my forthcoming book *Rascal the Dragon*, which is aimed at beginning readers. The drawings are known as roughs. Bob Lea provides these sketches to indicate his intended look for the characters and the layout of the story. If the author, editor or book designer requires changes (and they nearly always do) the artist does not have to rework the final, coloured, detailed drawings which can take days, weeks or even months for a single page.

I would like to use the story as an example as to how we might employ some of the strategies discussed so far. I will demonstrate with the child I have called Stefan again, who has already developed basic skills. For a complete beginner, read the story several times to the child over the course of a week or so. Let the child 'read' it back to you without stopping or correcting them. A more advanced reader than Stefan may only need one reading, to help them with the names of characters or the odd difficult word.

Remember, this is not a school reader. This is a proper book which is to be read for enjoyment. If your son or daughter can read it to themselves for the pure joy of it, then let them. It doesn't get any better than this. If you are going to be involved and listen to your child read aloud, do everything you can to make it easy and natural. It is not a lesson. It is reading a book together.

Cover and back cover
When you start the book mention the title in a natural way. You have already taught the two most common words – *Rascal* and *dragon*. Read the blurb on the back cover to see if the content sounds interesting. If it doesn't, find a book that does.

Title page and page 1
Mention the author and illustrator. Many children like particular authors and illustrators and will want to recognise their names.

You could read the first page to set up the words *dragon*, *loved* and *street*.

104

'Look at Sniff,' said Ben
'Isn't he great?'
'No,' said Dad. 'He smells.'
2
3

Pages 2 and 3
Let Stefan read these pages. The hardest words are *isn't*, *good* and *mine*. If Stefan doesn't get them immediately tell him what they are.

Notice that I have set up a pattern here which is repeated on the following pages, especially with the words *isn't* and *mine*.

'Look at Shovel,' said Ben.
'Isn't he great?'
'No,' said Dad. 'He digs holes.'
4
5

Pages 4 and 5
Shovel is the hardest word here along with *great* and *holes*. Before Stefan reads say something like, 'Oh, look at *Shovel*. He's digging holes.'

'Look at Ruff-Ruff,' said Ben.
'Isn't he great?'
'No,' said Dad. 'He barks.'
6
7

Pages 6 and 7
Stefan has a good chance of reading all of this except *terrific*. In subsequent reads, Stefan may confuse *good*, *great*, *terrific* and *fantastic* when he comes to them. Don't correct him.

Ruff-Ruff is easy to read and we will expect him to bark by now.

105

Reading for Meaning

Pages 8 and 9

Bomber is a difficult word but at this stage I would like to introduce a bit of fun. You might say, 'Oh, look at that dragon. Yuck, Stefan. Let's get another book.' You have introduced two hard words and I hope a howl of protest.

'Look at Bomber,' said Ben. 'Isn't he great?'

'No,' said Dad. 'He poos on people.'

8   9

Pages 10 and 11

Consider reading this pivotal page aloud yourself.

Talk about the emotional content. Every kid has been denied a pet.

Chapter 2

'Can I have a dragon, please Dad?' said Ben.

'No,' said Dad. He was cross because he could not start the fire.

10   11

Pages 12 and 13

Talk about your favourite dragon. Don't let Stefan try to sound out *played* because it is too hard. He might be able to guess it if he reads the rest of the sentence and goes back.

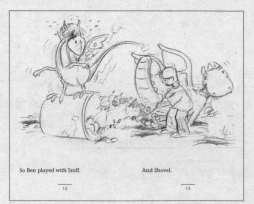

So Ben played with Sniff.   And Shovel.

12   13

106

And he played with Ruff-Ruff. 14

And Bomber. 15

Pages 14 and 15
With the pictures and the repetitive pattern Stefan should be able to read these pages.

Chapter 3

Just then, Ben saw a small stray dragon. It was wonderful. 16

'I wish you were mine,' said Ben. 'You are a little rascal.' 17

Pages 16 and 17
Read these pages aloud yourself or if you want Stefan to read, you could use the word *wonderful* in your own natural conversation to set it up.

The stray dragon followed Ben all the way home. 18

'Maybe Dad will let me keep you, Rascal,' said Ben. 19

Pages 18 and 19
Refer to the content. Will Dad do the right thing? Poor old Ben. Poor old Rascal. What will happen?

107

Reading for Meaning

Pages 20 and 21
These pages set up another repeating sequence. The drawings are funny and pre-empt the text on the next page. A good chance to have a talk about the naughty little dragon here. *Wash* is a new word but the picture should give a clue.

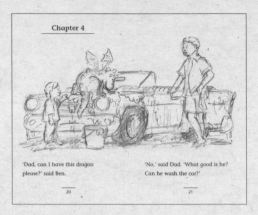

Chapter 4

'Dad, can I have this dragon please?' said Ben.

20

'No,' said Dad. 'What good is he? Can he wash the car?'

21

Pages 22 and 23
Just sit back with a delighted expression on your face and let Stefan read.

'No,' said Ben.

22

'Can he mow the lawn?'

23

Pages 24 and 25
Now we should really be rocking and rolling. We have an established pattern and repetition of the words except where the picture reveals new ones.

'No,' said Ben.

24

'Can he hang out the washing?'

25

108

Pages 26 and 27
Just sit back and enjoy.

Pages 28 and 29
What a wonderful illustration.

If Stefan reads *said* or *yelled* instead of *shouted*, ignore the substitution.

Page 30
Just talk about the story and then let Stefan read the whole book himself. Look pleased and if he reads yabber or gets the odd word wrong say nothing.

Good luck next time a stray dog comes by.

Just as a matter of interest – the little stories in the *Rascal* series are the most difficult I have written. They look easy but writing with few words is incredibly difficult. It is also great fun. Someone once said to me that I have the best job in the world. I would have to agree with that. But I am not the only person involved. May I also take this chance to pay tribute to my publisher, Julie Watts, who came up with the idea for *The Reading Bug* and a set of stories for young readers and sees them all through to books. Bob Lea, who illustrates the Rascal stories, and Andrew Weldon, who illustrated the book you are reading, contributed their wonderful artistic talents. Catherine McCredie edits the manuscripts with great love and Sandy Cull designs the books. Thanks, everyone.

7

Phonics

ghote spells fish

IN THIS CHAPTER

* What is phonics?
* What about Dr Seuss books?
* Why some children do well with the phonic method.
* Changing the alphabet.
* A few tips for those determined to use phonics.
* Phonics – *a* strategy, not *the* strategy.

'Dear Paul Jennings,' wrote a young fan. 'Please, please, please come to our school. Everyone will be raped if you do. Especially the English teachers.'

I must admit to having a chuckle. What a perfectly reasonable mistake. He had not yet learned the phonic rule that doubling the *p* makes the *a* short.

Phonics is a method of teaching reading based upon pronunciation of different letter combinations, such as *ch* or *sh*. It is one of the tools we use when we read. But it is a difficult tool to use and must be handled with care. There are two major problems. The first relates to the complexity of the system and the second to individual differences between children.

Phonic complexity

The mistake made by the little boy who wrote to me is understandable. He added *ed* to *rap. Rapt* is another alternative and would be more logical. Other spellings are *rapped* and even harder, *wrapped*. We have three meanings, one pronunciation and three spellings. *Wrapped*, like *rapt*, has four speech sounds (but seven letters). No wonder children come to realise that the system is unreliable.

Take an example we all understand: traffic lights. A red light means stop. An amber light means that red is about to appear and green means go. This is simple and it never changes. Now imagine a different situation. Here are some new rules:

* A red light means either stop or stop if there is another car near by.
* If a red light is accompanied by blue, give way only to four-wheel drive vehicles.
* In fine weather a red light may be ignored altogether.
* If a red light is accompanied by a blue light and a pink light, stop when the temperature is over thirty degrees Celsius.

Of course chaos, death and injury would result on the roads if we had such an inconsistent system. But the above example is a model of perfection compared to the phonic system in English.

114

THE PHONIC TRAFFIC LIGHT

There is an old joke amongst teachers – *ghote* spells *fish*.

The *f* comes from *gh* as in tou*gh*, the *i* sound comes from the *o* in w*o*men, the *sh* sound from the *t* in na*t*ion and the *e* is silent as in tam*e*.

Another favourite saying is, 'The *p* in *psalm* is silent as in *swimming*.'

(A silent pee in the pool.)

115

These jokes might be amusing to adults but it is not funny if you are a child learning to read. The relationship between the sounds and the letters in English is appalling. As a stand-alone method of teaching reading, phonics, which links sounds and letters, is problematic to say the least.

Sending a child off to decode words by sounding them out in isolation is a risky business. The chances of achieving a fit are extremely unlikely. Whatever rule you give the child will have a multitude of exceptions.

Consider the sound oo as in moon. There are twenty-three – yes, twenty-three – different ways of writing the sound oo in English:

oo as in moon	oup as in coup
u-e as in tune	iu as in jiujitsu
ui as in fruit	oeu as in manoeuvre
ew as in few	eu as in sleuth
$ough$ as in through	ous as in rendezvous
ou as in soup	ou-s as in mousse
ugh as in Hugh	ooh as in pooh
ui-e as in bruise	ue as in glue
wo as in two	u as in flu
oe as in canoe	u-e as in rule
ieu as in lieu	oo-e as in loose
o-e as in lose	

In addition, many of these letter combinations make other sounds – consider *book* and *moon* where *oo* represents two different sounds. Then take the word *through* and compare it with *tough*. Having done that, look at *bough* and compare it to *cow*. Some letters make no sound at all like the *b* in com*b* or the *k* in *k*nife. Having just taught the child that the first letter in *sit* makes a sound like a snake we present them with the word *sugar* where it is pronounced *sh* (and of course *c* also says *s* as in *c*ell). Some speech sounds have one letter to represent them such as the *d* in *d*og. Some have two like the *ch* in *ch*op. Or three like the *tch* in wa*tch*. Or even four such as the *ough* in thr*ough*.

THANK YOU
-COFF-
THANK YOU

THE COUGHING COW
BOWS ON THE BOUGH

117

Over the years there have been many different ways of using phonics in the teaching of reading. Some approaches try to present letters in such a way that the sound they make always stays the same. Words In Colour (Gattegno) is a scheme whereby the individual sounds are always printed in the same colour. For example the *s* sound in *kiss* and *sink* would be presented in a different colour to the *s* sound in *was* (which is *zzz*).

I used this system when I was training to be a special-school teacher. It is logical and I enjoyed using it. The main problems are the number of speech sounds in our language. The system covers fifty-three sounds (phonemes) and we don't have fifty-three colour names. Some of the combinations use two colours which look like stripes. The children have a large number of colour variations to link to particular sounds. Also, because of the complexity they tend to focus on sounds to the exclusion of other cueing systems.

The Initial Teaching Alphabet (Pitman) introduces symbols which resemble letters of the alphabet but are always used for the same speech sound. For example, this is the symbol for *sh*: ∫h. The children were weaned off these symbols as they gained confidence.

Other phonic schemes use storybooks which are limited to particular sounds. For example *pig, fig, jig, tig, rig* and *big* along with *can, fan, man, van, ban* and *ran*

might be the only words in the book. As you can imag
ine, it's hardly great literature.

It is possible to use stand-alone phonic reading
schemes, but I don't recommend them. The focusing of
attention on the structure of words and the insistence
on accuracy takes the pleasure out of reading. It also
denies the value of contextual clues and the meaning of
the passage. The child is focusing on the inside of words
rather than the content of the whole page or book. The
writer is also limited in the choice of vocabulary. The stories are usually stilted. And guessing based on meaning
is not allowed.

What about Dr Seuss books? Kids love them. They
are not really phonically controlled books. They use

119

rhyme and repetition and very funny, appealing stories. Take this example from *Green Eggs and Ham*:

> Would you like them in a house?
> Would you like them with a mouse?

It is the rhyming, repetition and use of wonderful illustrations which make these books very easy to read. The creature chasing around a poor character who does not want to eat green eggs and ham leads to loads of fun. A pure phonic reader using *house* and *mouse* would be unlikely to also include the word *would* in the text. Pure phonic readers are rarely fun.

The best way to use phonics is to include it as *one* of the strategies a child can use in figuring out the meaning of a passage (see Chapter 6).

Differences in children's abilities

There are complex processes involved in sounding out words. Some children will have natural ability, others will struggle. I love to play the button accordion but I have reluctantly come to the conclusion that I don't have a good ear for music. I would love to sit in with a group of friends at an Irish 'session' and play in the pub. But when the other musicians change key I don't notice until I see the glares and nods from the other players. I might as well face it – I will never be Sharon Shannon.

It is the same with sounding out words. Some children have problems. That which seems simple to us is really very complex. Here are a few of the steps down which a child might fall:

* Distinguishing the look of one letter from another (visual discrimination). The letter *s* is not *r*. This might seem easy but for some children it is not. The letters *p*, *b* and *d* are often confused.
* Remembering that you have seen that letter before (visual memory). It seems easy. How would you go remembering the appearance of these: なめちまった？ They are taken from the Japanese translation of my book *Unbearable*.
* Remembering which sound attaches to which letter (auditory visual association). Once again, easy for us but difficult for a young child.
* Distinguishing the sound of one letter from that of another (auditory discrimination). Like my inability to notice the changes of key in music, some children cannot tell the difference between the sound of *p* and *d*.

* Blending the individual sounds together in your head to make up a word (auditory synthesis). If you break up a word like *cat* into three speech sounds, *c-a-t*, some children will say *kitchen* or even *monkey* in response because to them when the word is broken up it sounds like gibberish.

There are children who cannot do one or more of the above tasks. It may be a maturational stage they will grow out of. On the other hand it may be a processing problem they are unable to overcome. The main thing for helpers is not to push the child into tasks they will fail at.

Handle with care

I am not against the use of phonics. I am against the abuse of it. Phonics is dynamite and must be handled with extreme care. If I had to point to one thing that has done more to put children off reading than anything else it would be the misuse of phonics.

I will also admit that in the days when I knew no better I taught my first daughter, Tracy, to read using phonically controlled books. She started school aged five with a reading age of eight years. She is now a fantastic reader and works as an editor. Does this indicate that phonics is the best method of reading instruction? No, it doesn't. Nor does anecdotal evidence supporting other methods of reading instruction.

Because it is such an emotional issue, supporters of various approaches to teaching reading often become enthusiasts, and sometimes, unfortunately, fanatics. You will not find a shortage of people who believe that phonics is the only method of teaching reading that works. At the most extreme they will reject nearly everything I have suggested in this book. Reading for meaning rather than word-for-word accuracy is heresy to some of these phonic 'purists'.

So how come my own daughter did so well on it?

There are a couple of factors involved. Tracy was one of those children who, for whatever reason, start off loving books. She had a wonderful vocabulary and had been read hundreds of storybooks by her mother and me. The language of books was second nature to her and she soon read her own choices which were proper books.

Secondly, she had a highly motivated teacher (me). Research shows that when you try to compare methods of reading used in schools there is a complicating factor that is hard to tease out – the enthusiasm and loving personality of the teacher.

A real enthusiast will arrive at school two hours

early and prepare work for the class. They will still be there at six o'clock at night. They go to conferences and seminars. They care about their children's feelings and individual needs. They are interesting, stimulating and passionate. They give papers and write books. They live for their students. Their students love them. Any method of teaching reading will work in the hands of such a person because they are totally in tune with their students' emotional needs and would never subject a child to the humiliation of sounding out a word which was beyond their ability.

If you get one of these teachers, no matter what their theoretical approach, you are on to something magical and marvellous. They account for the anecdotal success stories of methods which might otherwise seem problematic. And of course the influence of other factors such as the involvement of parents must also be considered.

I have said that I don't recommend phonics as a method of teaching reading on its own because the books which control phonic content are usually lacking in literary merit or fun. However, the relationship between the sounds and the letters still has a place in learning to read and spell. For parents helping a child to read unknown words, I suggest making it the last strategy to be employed, not the first.

There are three groups of clues or cueing systems which are available to a child when they try to read an unknown word. We have discussed the first two already in Chapter 6:

1 The likely meaning (semantics)

Children desperately want the word to make sense. They will not make a silly choice unless someone has taught them not to use meaning to help them 'guess'.

2 The natural order of words (syntax or grammar)

Intuitively, children know that a sentence like 'She was girl little a,' is incorrect. They do not expect *girl* after *was*.

3 The sounds associated with the letters (phonics or grapho-phonics)

The golden rule when handling this volatile material is the one I have been hammering all along. If it is fun, it is okay. If it is a struggle, it is dangerous. Simple. You can't do any harm if the child enjoys the activity. But you can put them off reading for life if the sounding out takes the joy out of books. Sounding out letters is not reading. Reading is getting meaning from print. If you feel uncertain about sounding out words, don't do it. You can still do an enormous amount to advance your child's progress without it.

Using these three systems, children will have a reasonable chance identifying a difficult word in the context of a story. Phonics should support not supplant the other two cueing systems.

A new alphabet?

The great playwright George Bernard Shaw offered a huge reward in his will to anyone who could get a phonically consistent spelling system adopted in England. Although the money was eventually shared out, his aim was never realised, and we are still left with an illogical alphabet. Imagine how easy it would be for everyone if *tough* was spelt *tuf* and *cell* was spelt *sel*.

There are reasons why some linguists object to the notion of one letter always representing the same sound. The first relates to units of meaning (morphemes) which can show the relationship between words. The words *sign* and *signature* are obviously related. The *g* would disappear from *sign* if we adopted a pure phonetic alphabet and the relationship between the two words would not be so obvious.

Another objection relates mainly to vowels which would be spelt differently according to your accent. A *fush* in New Zealand would be a different kettle of *fish* to one in Australia. But on the positive side, neither country would have *sh* because it would take just one letter to represent this sound so *fish* would have only three letters and three sounds which makes perfect sense.

My vote would be for changing the system. Making things easier for children, especially those experiencing difficulty, is the most critical factor. When I first started writing I had to remember whether *s* or *z* went on the end of words like surprise or realise. Now in Australia we can choose to use just *s* on most of these words (but not in the USA or UK). This is an improvement in consistency but I would have preferred to have used *z* because it is closer to what we actually pronounce.

Phonics can be useful. But until we change our alphabet it will be an unreliable tool.

Take a group of letters, put them together and what have you got?

In most cases a struggling reader will tell you – nuthing that mayks eny cence.

Phonic fun

I am not going to include a sequence for teaching phonics. There are tens of thousands of these programs available. Another one would be redundant.

GREAT WORD-FUN BOOKS

Primary

I'm Talking Big
Colin McNaughton

The Phantom Tollbooth
Norton Juster, Jules Feiffer (illus.)

Sky in the Pie
Roger McGough, Satoshi Kitamura (illus.)

Teaching phonic combinations in isolation can cause problems if it is done in a boring way. Simply barking out letters is usually not much fun. There are books, however, which use jokes and riddles and puzzles as word play. Children read these by choice for the very reason that they are fun.

Here is an example from *Spit It Out*, a book I have written with Terry Denton and Ted Greenwood. Spoonerisms, in which sounds have been mixed up, are great fun to work out. Readers are provided a list of phrases (in this instance: *bee on the peak*, *socks on feet*, *case of rats* and *boating fleas*) and accompanying illustrations to help them work out the spoonerisms:

Case of rats is meant to be *race of cats*. You can work out the rest. Riddles, puns and spoonerisms involve phonics but they are great fun and create positive rather than negative feelings.

If you are determined to teach the relationship between the sounds and the letters, by all means go ahead. But here are a few tips:

* Keep it fun. Make you own board games with letters written on them. Have a fantastic time so that your child can't wait to do it again.
* Remember that recognising a letter with no other clues is a difficult task. Consider the following:

What is this? ☂ A picture of an umbrella.

What is this? ☂ Another picture of an umbrella, this time turned upside down.

What is this? d The letter *d*.

What is this? p The letter *d* turned upside down? No, it is the letter *p*.

An umbrella stays an umbrella but a *d* is not always a *d*.

* Some children take a long time to realise that letters, unlike umbrellas, can't be turned back to front or upside down.

129

* Watch for signs of frustration and boredom. Read the child's non-verbal signals. Are they having a good time?
* If too many words are unknown, then the book or activity is not suitable. Find something easier.
* Make sure that children get 95 per cent of their attempts correct. There is nothing like failure to create avoidance. Success breeds success.
* If the child reads *p-i-t* and cannot blend it into the word *pit*, give the activity up. It is too difficult. If they don't get it quickly, tell them the word and move on.
* Don't add an additional sound after *p*, *t* or *k*. It is not *puh-i-tuh* but *p-i-t*. (Try whispering *p* and *t*.)
* Don't pronounce the *r* on the end of words. *Car* only has two speech sounds unless you live in America or Scotland. In the days when we were importing American teachers into Australia we had infants sounding like George Bush.

Remember, phonics is just a small part of reading. Don't forget all the other wonderful strategies such as reading past the word for additional clues. These may be a lot more useful than phonics.

8

Personal Writing

The magnifesent dinasaw

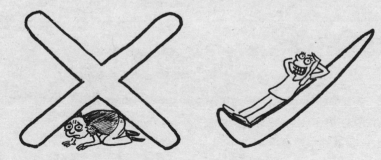

IN THIS CHAPTER

* Personal writing is a great way to teach reading.
* Why would a child feel any less dejected about their forgotten pieces of writing than I feel about my bottom drawer of rejected manuscripts?
* Some great writing activities.
* Elective spelling.
* Text messaging.
* More ticks, please.
* Look, cover, write, check.
* Risk-taking in writing.

When my first book, *Unreal*, was published I was so proud of it that I carried a copy around with me for weeks. I would sneak a look at it every now and again and proudly say to myself, 'I wrote that.'

It had been an enormous effort. Writing in my spare time on weekends. Sending manuscripts to publishers. Acceptance. Then rewriting and editing and waiting for the final result. So much of me had gone into that collection of stories that I worried I might die and miss all the pleasure of seeing it published.

What every author wants

There is nothing quite like one's first book but I still get a thrill when I receive the author's advance copy of a new title. It is my reward. It is tangible evidence of my personal struggle.

I have written manuscripts for stories which have not been published and there is no thrill at all. Just a feeling of time wasted and disappointment. I want my work to be read. Every author does.

Including children.

If we remember this simple proposition, we can make personal writing a rewarding experience for our kids. Go about it the right way and they will love putting pen to paper. And when they write, of course, they read. Personal writing is a great way to teach reading.

In schools, many teachers use the same processes with children that adult writers use. Particularly for a major piece of work like a story or a book.

This usually involves getting an idea, writing an outline, discussion with a teacher or friend, writing a rough draft, editing, rewriting or typing, illustrating and publishing in a bound or stapled form. All the celebratory parts such as a book launch are added.

In less-informed times teachers would give children a topic like 'My Holiday', set them writing, correct the mistakes and that was it. No wonder the kids hated it. They had the cake with no icing. Why would a child feel any less dejected about these forgotten pieces of writing than I feel about my bottom drawer of rejected manuscripts?

It is now recognised that children's writing must have purpose and joy and validity. When they participate in this creative process they are improving their reading and spelling skills enormously.

And enjoying it.

When a child looks at their own writing they are reading material which has spelling mistakes. This doesn't necessarily diminish its value. When the final product has a use or purpose, the child is usually happy to be included in correcting the mistakes. With a long piece of writing the parent could type up the piece, correcting the spelling mistakes as their contribution. A computer spellchecker, while not foolproof, can help too.

Probably most parents will want to leave full-blown

135

YOU CALL THEM MISTAKES, I CALL THEM 'CREATIVE EXPRESSION'

publishing efforts to the schools although some children are so keen about writing that they would love to make books at home with the assistance of their parents. And remember that home-made books do not always have to be fiction. Many kids are experts on subjects like space exploration or body-surfing and would enjoy writing descriptions, instructions and informative texts about these subjects. They might also like to write about themselves. Anne Frank's *The Diary of a Young Girl*, written by a teenager, is probably one of the most powerful books ever written. In a lighter vein, *Penny Pollard's Diary*, a fictional story by Robin Klein, is a great motivator to record some of the funnier moments in life.

Great activities

There are many other uses for everyday writing that are valuable and full of enjoyment but require less effort. Writing that has a purpose related to everyday living is not seen as work. We should make the best of these wonderful opportunities to get children writing. Collectively, they are learning-experiences of extraordinary value.

Here are some of my favourites.

1   Diaries or journals

Most children need diaries for school and organising their social lives. They enjoy listing birthdays (especially their own), the names of friends, sporting events, holidays and exciting happenings. Many like to record the past day or week so that they can look back on it in future years. I encourage children to turn their diaries into time capsules to be opened in twenty years time. The children include pictures of friends, train tickets, certificates and other mementos of the year.

Kids love diaries – they are reading and writing without being subjected to lessons.

Some children love keeping a journal – a book in which recollections are recorded. Journals which record important experiences and the emotional reactions to them are very popular with some children.

137

Fancy journals with locks are available, as are diaries by popular writers, sporting figures and show business personalities.

2 Letters

Most children enjoy writing letters, especially to loved ones like grandparents. If they receive answers quickly the correspondence can go on for long periods of time with benefits to both parties. One of my grandchildren, aged nine, began writing to the elderly lady next door who thoroughly enjoyed the process and the contact with her young admirer. The main benefit from an exchange like this is probably the human contact but letters like these are a great way to encourage reading.

3 Cookbooks

Copying out favourite recipes and actually using them to cook is a great idea. They can be kept in an exercise book and revisited often.

4 Holiday maps and plans

Kids love holidays. Let them research the journey and find places to stop or stay. The locations of favourite food stops are always interesting. Children can construct maps and give directions to the driver as the journey commences. These could then be pasted into diaries or journals.

5 Family trees

Everyone likes to have a family context for their life. Listing parents, grandparents, cousins and other relations is a fun activity with meaning. Birthdates, deaths and occupations can be appended. A family tree can be extended by including interesting events and anecdotes. A visit to a cemetery can be very illuminating and is not necessarily a bleak experience. Reading a gravestone is still reading.

6 Collections

Children love to collect. It doesn't really matter what the subject of the collection is. It may be dolls, model cars, swap cards, books, tokens, autographs or photos of sporting figures. Because collections generate such enthusiasm the notion of making written lists, charts and wish lists is very appealing to kids and a great reading activity into the bargain.

7   Presents

Ask any child to write a list of what they want for Christmas. You will not be disappointed at the quality of the vocabulary attempted. When they are giving presents to others make sure they attach name tags with messages of love on each.

8   Television

Having decided on a reasonable amount of television to be watched give the children the task of listing the times and names of the favourite programs. Be prepared to negotiate.

MY PARENTS' POLICY IS IF IF YOU CAN SPELL IT, YOU CAN WATCH IT. I GET TO WATCH 'E.R.' BUT NOT 'BANANAS IN PYJAMAS'.

9 Shopping lists

Write down your items then ask the kids to add their own. Re-write or type the list with correct spelling and take the children with you to search out the items in the supermarket. There is a lot of fun and reading involved in this activity.

10 Timetables

Work out a timetable for each day and pin it up in the kitchen. If you have a yearly planner put the children's interests on it as well as your own.

11 Advertisements

Selling something? Want to buy something? Get the kids to help you write the ads.

12 Rules

All families and societies need rules to govern themselves. These can be general or relate to specific situations, such as how to behave when travelling in the car (who gets to sit in the front seat on which days, no fighting et cetera) or who gets to use the canoe on holidays. These rules can be negotiated and written up by the children. They can also include rules for the parents, for example: 'Dad will not go to the toilet just when the washing-up is about to be done.'

13 Party lists

If you are organising a birthday party, don't do it all yourself. Get the children to make a list of everyone to be invited. Ask them to write out the invitations and address them. They can help plan the games and write down the program. List the menu and favourite foods. Put out place names – if you are worried about the spelling, ask the children to do rough drafts and then correct them before the final artistic efforts.

14 Personalised photo albums

This idea mirrors an activity which many adults use (always a good sign of a meaningful task). The children select a range of photographs, paste them into their own book and write subtitles and anecdotes about the photos.

Special events such as birthdays, holidays and funny incidents are particularly involving.

15   Memoirs

'Tell me about when I was a baby, Mum.' 'What was it like when you were a kid, Dad?' Children love the funny and unusual stories that make up family folklore. Compile a book of them to which everyone can contribute. Put a pen and pad next to the phone and record funny events and conversations.

16   E-mails and text messaging

E-mails and text messaging are here to stay. They are legitimate forms of writing and communicating.

SIMON, WHERE'S YOUR HOMEWORK ASSIGNMENT?

I SMSD IT 2 U MS

Personal writing is not work, because it has an enjoyable and valuable function in everyday life. It has value beyond measure. Your children will learn without knowing it. Fantastic stuff.

UR OOL if U can't spel

In the days when I was a teachers' college lecturer, the Victorian Teachers' Union put out a bumper sticker that read as follows:

IF YOU CAN READ THIS THANK A PRIMARY SCHOOL TEACHER.

A wit on our staff produced her own version and bet me that I wouldn't put it on my car. She was right. There was no way I was going out to visit students and teachers with a message saying:

IF YOU CAN REED THIS THANK A PRIMARY SCHOOL TEECHER.

The bumper sticker was funny but it underscores an interesting point. People think spelling is important, especially employers, teachers and editors. I remember once taking a mark off a top student's essay because she had a spelling mistake on the first line. She was mortally offended and went on and on and on about it. Even now, twenty years later, she is still annoyed. After eighteen years of marriage and all we have been through, she hasn't forgotten how picky I was.

Although we joke that I married her to shut her up, in a way Claire is right. Spelling is only important because we think it is. The ideas are much more significant than the spelling. In Shakespeare's time spelling was optional. In those days you could even spell a word differently on the same page. As long as readers could recognise the word it didn't matter.

KEEPING THINGS POSITIVE

UM... YOUR WRITING HAS A SHAKESPEARIAN QUALITY TO IT...

145

But now we have no choice. Accuracy, unfortunately, is essential. If your job application contains a spelling mistake, you probably won't get the job.

Having said this, recent developments with mobile phones may indicate that a change is coming. Users of SMS text messages are using acronyms such as KISS (keep it simple stupid) and OOL (out of luck). I received a letter the other day using the numeral 4 instead of *for* and the letter *U* instead of *you*. This imaginative shorthand may become acceptable in a wide range of communications.

The use of e-mails in offices is also having an effect on our standards. Some people receive hundreds of messages every day, most requiring replies. Spelling mistakes (usually typing errors) are allowed to pass because the writer

146

is frantically trying to cope with the load. I was initially amazed to receive e-mails containing numerous mistakes from editors who are trained to pounce on every one.

If elective spelling results from these changes, I will not have any complaints. For the moment, however, correct spelling is required in most occupations.

A lifetime effort

If you read the chapter on phonics, you will see how difficult it is for kids to learn to spell accurately. And as I point out, phonics is an extremely unreliable guide.

Learning to spell correctly is a lifetime effort. I will be quite honest about it – I am not a great speller. Fortunately, I have the luxury of an editor to check my work. And of course, spellcheckers on computers are a good (but not perfect) guide.

This book is about the reading bug and not the spelling bee. Reading and spelling are separate and different skills. Maybe my next book will be about spelling. But here are a few general observations which may help you to put spelling in context.

Keep everything positive. I recall one of my children bringing home a piece of creative writing which had thirty-two red crosses on one page. I visited the teacher and politely pointed out that there were no ticks, only crosses. 'We only mark the mistakes,' she said.

Imagine how the child feels to have all the mistakes and none of the good bits recognised.

Even now, after thirty books, and years of writing, I still need my editor's affirmation. I groan when I see hundreds of pencil notations in the margin. I know it sounds pathetic but authors need praise. My editor, Julie Watts, will always start off with, 'It's a terrific story, Paul. I especially like . . .'

I *want* her to point out the mistakes. I *need* her to point out the mistakes. But I am much more interested in what she thinks about the content. And I hate it when she tells me a story is no good. I want to hear that it is fantastic.

If a mature (?) and experienced writer needs this reinforcement, imagine how much more a child does.

Always make sure that you have more good things to say about a child's work than bad. Make sure there are more ticks than crosses. Respond to the content of a child's writing in a big way. Let them down gently with the spelling.

If your son or daughter brings home a list of words to learn, keep it fun. The Look, Cover, Write, Check method is a popular strategy with teachers. *Write* the word down while you are looking at the correct spelling.

Cover it up. *Write* it down again. *Check* to see if you are right. If you are not, do it again.

And don't forget that there are dictionaries specially written and illustrated for children. They can be used to help find correct spellings. Another good idea is to make a personal dictionary.

GREAT FIRST DICTIONARIES

Oxford First Illustrated Dictionary
Emma Chichester-Clark (illus.)

My Very First Personal Dictionary (Oxford)

Dictionary (DK)

Another of my favourite strategies is to let the child go through the same process as the adult author. Let them write a rough draft and forget about the spelling. It is wonderful what they can come up with if they are allowed to. A risk-taker who writes 'The magnifesent dinasaw croucht on its loffty perch,' is making much more progress than the fearful writer who comes up with, 'The cat sat on the mat.'

149

When the rough draft is finished you could say, 'Susan, why don't you put a circle around all the words you think might be spelt incorrectly?'

After this, you can both have a bit of fun trying to find out the correct spelling. Whatever you do, remember the golden rules. Keep it fun. And make sure that the child succeeds and does not experience failure and struggle.

9

Visual Literacy

The picture tells it all

IN THIS CHAPTER

* A cartoon has a voice of its own.
* Non-verbal language can be great fun.
* Kids love reading pictures.
* The illustrator tells part of the story.
* Without words the reader is moved to tears.
* They always draw the doctor as a man.
* Pictures are enormous influences in our lives.

When is an illustrator not an illustrator? Answer: nearly always. Most illustrators do not just draw pictures of objects or events in the text. They nearly always make comments of their own. Have a look at the cartoon by Andrew Weldon on page 151, which is a humorous introduction to this chapter. This cartoon is a very clever comment on my ideas. It has a voice of its own. I asked my publisher to find me an artist who would do this because it adds so much to the book when another person contributes a visual comment rather than simply illustrating what I have written.

Reading the pictures

Learning to read visual symbols other than words is an important part of becoming literate. Some people are better at it than others but it is a skill which can be taught, particularly in relation to picture books.

The world is full of symbols and children start to recognise many of them very early in their lives. The big *M* of McDonald's is a brilliant marketing symbol. Children under two years of age know that it means food years before they realise it is a letter of the alphabet. They sense the excitement in the car as their brothers and sisters point to the golden arches, and then groan as their father or mother drives past.

HE'S STARTING TO LEARN THE ALPHABET. HE ALREADY KNOWS K, F, C & M.

Another well-known sign – the red circle with a bar through it – warns of a prohibition. No smoking. No horses. No dogs. In a clever application of this symbol an insightful publicist placed it across a ghost. Every child immediately associated the sign with the movie *Ghostbusters*. What a great marketing device. Advertising agencies understand visual literacy. So do all good teachers. Interpreting non-verbal language is a part of

154

learning to read, not just in books but also in the world around us. And it can be great fun.

In the popular picture book *Where the Wild Things Are*, author-illustrator Maurice Sendak tells the story of Max, who leaves his bed to visit an island inhabited by monsters. He has great adventures there which seem to involve a long stay. When he finally returns to his bedroom we wonder how long he was gone for. Was it just a dream or did many hours or days pass? Did any of it really happen? Ask a class of children and someone will always notice what I did not when I first read the story. The moon outside his window is now full and has entered another phase. Many days have passed. Kids love this sort of analysis and can become extremely good at reading pictures in books.

Unlike Maurice Sendak, most authors cannot draw well. I am hopeless and always need the help of an illustrator. Together we write the picture book. The illustrator tells part of the story. This is why most picture books cannot be read on the radio. In our book, *The Fisherman and the Theefyspray*, Jane Tanner tells her part of the story with pictures. The story is about the last Theefyspray fish in the world. The poor creature is about to become extinct when a wonderful event occurs. A baby Theefyspray is born. As readers we do not want this baby to die. But we are worried. Jane has drawn a shadow on the surface of the water which we later realise is a boat. Then we see a

155

hook with bait. The text does not mention either of these things. Finally, in an incredibly dramatic picture, we see the baby take the hook. There are no words on this page. They are not needed. The picture tells it all.

Jane modified her drawings to suit my story in a number of ways. And I changed the text at her request. I will always remember her indignant phone call when she came to work on the page which read, 'He threw the Theefyspray back.'

'Paul,' she said. 'That is so like a man. Write, "He *put* the Theefyspray back."' I did, and Jane drew a magnificent picture of two gnarled hands gently lowering the Theefyspray back into the water.

He put the Theefyspray back.

My experience is that most artists do not like to be given illustration briefs from the author. Although Jane and I discussed the need for her drawings to show the threat of the fisherman she really did not want anything

156

more from me. 'It's my baby now, Paul,' she said. 'You leave it with me.'

It's a little like movie directors. They do not like to be told where to put the camera. When I wrote my first script for the television series 'Round the Twist', I read a book about camera angles, panning and zooming and all the rest of it. I peppered the script with all the terms, showing off my knowledge. The script came back with a terse note from the director. 'You get on with telling the story and let me decide how to shoot it.' In all the twenty-six scripts I wrote for this series I never mentioned the camera again.

There is an interesting similarity between television programs and picture books. In one of my early scripts I wrote a piece of dialogue where one of the children said, 'Look at that old sea chest washed up on the shore down there.' It came back from the editor with the whole line crossed out. He replaced it with one word – 'Look.' Picture books often work the same way.

In the end, however, it is up to the author to make sure that the illustrations and the words work together to help the reader understand the text. My publisher, Julie Watts, asked me to write four introductory storybooks for beginning readers. These books, about a world where dragons replace dogs, revolve around a little stray called Rascal. In this case, because the pictures tell so much of the story, I wrote a detailed illustration brief for the artist, Bob Lea. Opposite is the first page of it as modified by my book designer, Sandy Cull. The rough on page 104 is a later development.

I have asked that the main parts of the picture not fall into the gutter between the pages. This is important for double-page spreads so that the lovely artwork doesn't have a crease down the middle.

Matching text and illustrator

I have worked with a number of illustrators and they all have tremendous talents and ranges in what they are able to draw. Certain features of their work have appealed to me as suiting particular stories. Keith McEwan shows chaotic facial expressions and movement in his work. Peter Gouldthorpe is able to convey a wonderful sense of foreboding and mysticism. Craig Smith depicts the whimsical humour of domestic life perfectly. Jane Tanner conveys powerful emotion even without showing a face: she is a passionate person and she illustrates passionately. Terry Denton has a wicked sense of humour. He pushes the fun to the absolute limit in an inimitable way. Some authors might not like an illustrator inserting as much of their own humour into the stories as Terry does, but I love it. Bob Lea is up with the very latest techniques

Book One

Rascal the Dragon

Artist's brief

The central joke of these four books is that dragons exist like dogs and fulfil all the doggy functions. This peculiarity goes unremarked. The behaviour of the dragons is what makes them doggy not their appearance which is very dragon-like. Everything else in the world is normal. The dragons are named Sniff (he is smelly and sniffs around and is followed by a cloud of flies), Shovel (digs holes), Ruff-Ruff (barks), and Bomber (drops poo from the sky). The same dragons will re-appear in subsequent titles. Mind no characters or main action appears in the gutter.

Text	Illustrations	Characters
Ben loved dragons.	Ben sitting on ground maybe wearing a dragon T-shirt or a dragon tail, roaring like one with his hands up like claws (like a tiger). We see Sniff's shadow coming in from the right hand side.	Ben **Props** dragon tail shadow

159

GREAT BOOKS CONTAINING PUZZLING PICTURES

Pre-school

A Dark, Dark Tale
Ruth Brown

Primary

Where the Forest Meets the Sea
Jeannie Baker

Gorilla
Anthony Browne

Where's Wally?
Martin Handford

Willy's Pictures
Anthony Browne

How to Live Forever
Colin Thompson

Wolf!
Sara Fanelli

Dog's Night
Meredith Hooper and Alan Curless

in computer-generated art. His use of perspective is incredible and the dragon characters he has created for the Rascal books are wonderfully original.

Interpreting visual symbols

Some picture books have no words at all. These can be valuable to both accomplished and struggling readers. Raymond Briggs' *The Snowman* is a wonderful graphic novel about a snowman who comes to life and then begins to melt. It can move the reader to tears – all without words. Other popular titles are *Window* by Jeannie Baker and *Clown* by Quentin Blake.

Wordless picture books can be used to lift the esteem of reluctant readers who have difficulty with text. These books may not directly teach the recognition of words but they still have many uses. The child learns to start at the beginning and move towards the back of the book. And they learn that stories have structure and

DO YOU HAVE ONE LIKE THIS BUT WITHOUT ANY WORDS?

move from one event to another. They are telling a tale, albeit without words. They help children to predict and interpret. They teach visual literacy. And most importantly, they lead children to associate books with pleasure. They are fun.

Reading maps is an important visual literacy task. Children can read maps for us when we drive. Give them the map and let them direct you. Nadia Wheatley and Donna Rawlins produced a lovely book called *My Place* which has maps integrated into the text.

Visual literacy takes many forms. I once worked with a ten-year-old boy who had serious reading problems. He could not even recognise simple words like *pig* and *man*. Then one day he arrived for his session early and found me trying to set the time on a new digital watch. I was frustrated to the point of throwing the silly thing into the bin. It had four buttons which beeped but seemed totally unrelated to anything on the little screen.

I THINK AFTER WE'VE COVERED VISUAL LITERACY WE'RE GOING TO GO BACK OVER 'LEFT' & 'RIGHT'

GLUG GLG GLG

James took the watch from my hand without a word and in a few seconds had set the date, time and alarm.

I am hopeless with these gadgets. Video machines, microwaves and computer games are total enigmas. I used to say that the people who wrote the manuals were illiterate but I have to face the fact that I am not skilled in these particular forms of visual literacy. My secretary has to program numbers into my mobile phone because I can't do it myself.

Children have differences in their abilities too. There seem to be both individual and gender factors involved. There is a popular saying that boys are good at reading maps and throwing balls and that girls are good at everything else. This is an exaggeration, of course, but there is some truth in it. As a group, girls are better readers and writers than boys. There are more boys who struggle with reading than girls. But girls are not as adept at some perceptual manipulative tasks.

Even though more boys than girls read my books, I get far more letters from girls. This is partly because girls write more letters than boys do, but it also reflects their general superiority and interest in linguistic tasks.

Boys are more at risk for reading problems. They are also very sensitive in regard to the relationship between their perceived masculinity and the reading task. They do not want to be seen as nerds or bookworms. There is evidence that while a girl will happily buy a book with a boy on the cover, a boy will probably not buy a book with a girl on the cover. This is a particularly disturbing aspect of visual literacy and one which must be addressed.

IS THAT A BOY OR A GIRL DOLPHIN? BECAUSE IF IT'S A GIRL I'M NOT INTERESTED.

FLIPPY THE DOLPHIN

It is critical that we as parents, and society as a whole, present books as high-status objects and writing as a high-prestige activity for both boys and girls. This is why I have never refused to sign an autograph. Kids need to have writers, dancers, artists and poets as heroes and heroines as well as actors, football players and soldiers. J.K. Rowling – good on you for raising the status of authors.

The visual interpretation of pictures in books is a great way to head off these gender (and other) biases in our culture. My wife, Claire, has written several books on storytelling and reading instruction. When she works with children she often uses a picture book called *Ca-a-r, Ca-a-a-a-r* by Geoff Havel and Peter Kendall, to great effect. The seemingly simple story is about a driver who loses control, causes mayhem on a farm and finally injures himself. Claire stops at the page that reads, *'Quack,' said the duck as the doctor climbed out of the ambulance.* She reads the text but she doesn't show the page. Instead, she asks the children to draw the illustration themselves.

They always draw the doctor as a man.

This type of activity can lead to great discussions without involving a sermon.

Authors and artists do make mistakes. I was involved in a shameful incident which still makes me

164

blush. The producer of 'Round the Twist' asked me to meet an executive from an American television station. The executive was thinking of taking the series on his network but he had a problem with it. The three of us met for breakfast and the executive, an African-American, came straight to the point. 'Paul,' he said, 'there are no black people in this show. There are no Aborigines. Nor are there any Asians, Indians or any other children from the many cultural groups in Australia.'

I was shocked. It was like being hit with a hammer. How had we allowed this to happen? I wasn't in charge of casting but I had a say. Why hadn't I noticed? It was particularly terrible because there are Aboriginal people in my own family. The show was made a long time ago but there was no excuse. We made sure the same thing didn't happen in the next series.

As they grow older, children who are taught to critically read the pictures (and the text) will notice the mistakes and biases in pictures, books and movies. They will read the good, intentional messages of the artists and also perceive the weaknesses, omissions and tricks. They will become aware of insidious practices such as product placement in movies. They will know that it is not accidental when the main scene in a movie takes place in front of a giant poster of a popular soft drink. They learn to become critical viewers and recognise the tricky strategies that are used in politics and advertising, particularly on television.

Pictures are enormous influences in our lives. Learning to read them can start early.

The Bible starts with the sentence, 'In the beginning was the Word.' While it is probably true that humans spoke before they drew pictures, it is also true that they communicated with pictures on cave walls long before they wrote words. Visual literacy has had a major place in the growth of the human race. Today it remains an incredibly important part of a child's education. A part in which parents can play the leading role.

166

10

The Reluctant Reader

Good books grab

IN THIS CHAPTER

* Search for something of great interest to your child.
* Motivation is the key.
* Attitude is everything.
* Everyone likes to laugh.
* Where is the book that is easy to read and looks sophisticated?
* You can find books that will satisfy a grade-six child with grade-two reading skills.
* Dealing with learning disorders.

'I'm sick of these piddly little books about motorbikes,' shouted my then nine-year-old son, with tears in his eyes. I had been sitting in front of the fire listening to him read. He was a reluctant reader and I had chosen a nice, easy remedial story with a lot of pictures to help him guess the words. The book went flying across the room.

I picked up the remedial reader and examined it. Sure, it was about some teenagers with motorbikes. And he was interested in motorbikes which was why I had chosen it. But nothing of interest happened in the story. There was no plot. No tension, no mystery, no humour. Just a tiny little incident about some kids helping a farmer.

My first reaction was shame. Because I had shamed my son. He was embarrassed to be seen with such a book. He was bored with it. He was humiliated by it. I was reminded of my early teaching days when *John and Betty* was a text. I can remember wondering why they just hop, hop, hopped. Why didn't they fall down

169

the well or break a leg? Why wasn't there a story? Incredibly, you can start reading *Janet and John* from the back to the front and it makes no difference because no page is related to any other page.

My second reaction was, 'I think I could write a better story than that.'

That is how I came to write my first non-educational book, *Unreal*, back in 1984. I worked very hard to tell a good story in simple prose. I wrote short stories with surprise endings to give the readers a quick reward. I even put chapters inside the short stories to give convenient stopping points. I knew humour was a sought-after ingredient. Everyone likes to laugh – especially kids. Basically,

I wanted to appeal to ten- to thirteen-year-olds with reading delays of up to three years.

Getting rid of the stigma

For the book to work with the reluctant reader, it must attract the good reader as well, then there will be no stigma attached to being seen with it.

Not every child likes my books. Thank goodness for individual differences. You know your child's likes and dislikes better than anyone else. Search for something of great interest to them. As mentioned earlier, there are fiction and non-fiction books and magazines on practically

every subject. Is it football, cars, computers, netball, stamps, surfing or horses? Motivation is the key. Kids will fight to understand if they love the content.

In the fiction area humorous books by Andy Griffiths are popular (e.g. *Just Crazy!*, *Just Tricking!*). Emily Rodda writes easy-to-read fantasy (*The Deltora Quest* and *Rowan of Rin* series). Morris Gleitzman writes humorously and explores social issues (*Two Weeks with the Queen*) as does Anne Fine with *Madam Doubtfire*. Roald Dahl is an old favourite (*The BFG*) and Jeremy Strong, author of *The Hundred-Mile-an-Hour Dog*, is growing in popularity. E.B. White's *Charlotte's Web* is a very easy to read and moving story for mid-primary-school children.

If a book is boring to certain children we face the danger of turning them off. When I read a novel to myself I give it thirty or forty pages before I decide not to continue. Nobody forces me to finish it. Children will probably go three or four pages before reaching the same decision. Don't make them continue – find another book.

The main obstacle with most reluctant readers is that they have come to dislike books. Either the subject matter has been inappropriate or they have had failure experiences.

Failure experiences fall into two types. The first is when the subject matter is incomprehensible to the child. The concepts are too difficult and the story or other content

has no meaning. The second is when the words themselves take too much time to decode and the struggle to read each one takes away the enjoyment.

Our task with reluctant readers is to reverse the perception of failure. This in itself can be difficult but the situation is compounded when a child has an actual reading ability that is well below the child's age. As the gap between reading ability and actual age becomes wider it is more and more difficult to find a book which the child *can* read and *wants* to read. The child may be in grade six and only able to read books at a grade-two level. This is a dangerous situation and we need to give the child assistance without delay.

Let's address the main obstacle first. How the child feels about books.

Have you ever had one of those dreams where you are walking down the street and are practically naked? You stretch that T-shirt down to cover your private bits but it is just too skimpy. Total humiliation, embarrassment and panic overwhelm you. In a dream it is horrifying. In real life it is unbearable.

That's how the child in grade six who can only read little kids' books feels. Totally exposed. If everyone else is reading a fat book that looks like a novel, we cannot ask a child to carry around a thin book with babyish illustrations. It is totally embarrassing. I know I am hammering this point but the child's attitude is everything.

'Okay,' you say, 'so where is the book that is easy to read and looks sophisticated?' A good question. My own short stories have reading difficulty levels of around eight or nine years as far as the difficulty of the words and sentences are concerned. The conceptual difficulty varies from book to book. Generally speaking I would grade them as follows from easiest to most challenging:

* The Rascal books (*Rascal the Dragon* etc., forthcoming) interest level 3–6 years.
* The Cabbage Patch books (*The Cabbage Patch Fib* etc.) interest level 6–10 years.

* The Singenpoo stories (*The Paw Thing* etc.)
  interest level 7–10 years.
* The Gizmo books (*Come Back Gizmo* etc.) interest
  level 8–11 years.
* The short-story collections (*Unreal* etc.) interest
  level 9–14 years.

Conceptually, I have aimed straight at the ages shown above but the actual reading difficulty level is anything up to two years below this. In some cases more. I don't allow these reading levels to be put on the book because the stories are not remedial in nature. They are easy to read but have appropriate themes for good readers. An

GREAT, EASY-TO-READ, FUN BOOKS

Funny books

The Killer Underpants
Michael Lawrence

The Hundred-Mile-an-Hour Dog
Jeremy Strong

A diary

Utterly Me, Clarice Bean
Lauren Child

A book of letters

Little Wolf's Book of Badness
Ian Whybrow, Tony Ross (illus.)

A rude book

Mummy Never Told Me
Babette Cole

A book of wordplay

Firewords
John Foster

A weird book

The Bad Beginning (1st of *A Series of Unfortunate Events*)
Lemony Snicket

author has to attract good readers in order for the story to be a real story and for the book to be a real book.

You are going to have to search for more titles by other authors. Many of the books listed in Chapter 13 have a higher interest level than reading level.

The further behind a child is, the more difficult it becomes to find the right book. A child in grade six with grade-two skills is going to be hard to satisfy. But it can be done. A few examples are listed on this page.

There will be those of you who feel, 'This is all very well but my child has something wrong with him or her. My child has a special learning disorder and that is why he or she can't read.' You may well be right and I always think that parents' anxieties should be fully explored.

Dyslexia is going around

Once when I was waiting at the school gate to pick up my six-year-old daughter I couldn't help overhearing two mothers speaking. The first said to the second, 'I'm taking my child out of this school because dyslexia is going around.'

I kept my counsel. Perhaps I should have said something. But dyslexia is not something that can be caught like a cold. There is no doubt that there is a group of children who have specific learning difficulties related to perceptual, cognitive or linguistic factors. As a speech therapist I spent many years working with them. Most children who have reading difficulties, however, do not suffer from these problems. In some cases early maturational delay is a factor (see Chapter 5).

Most reluctant readers have attitudinal, social or environmental reasons for their problem. The great majority have fallen behind because they see books as bad, and reading as ridiculous. They have had hurtful experiences. It is not a case of once bitten twice shy. It is a thousand times bitten. And now terrified.

If you are worried about perceptual or neurological problems, go to a recommended specialist. Start looking for help at your school and take a referral from an educational psychologist or trained reading teacher. Be careful of fanciful schemes from enthusiasts who recommend easy solutions like spectacles with pink lenses.

If you do decide to bring in a specialist, make sure that you ask questions. You want a person who cares about the feelings and interests of the child. You want someone who knows the books and is a good listener. Too often we hand things over to experts like doctors, lawyers and psychologists without question. Finding the right specialist is important.

Start at your school and take recommendations. Most education departments have educational psychologists, speech therapists or reading specialists. If they have waiting lists and you suspect your child has a severe learning or perceptual problem, ask for recommendations or referrals to other specialists.

My first class was known as an Opportunity Grade. I had fifteen children in my care, which was considered a small number in those days of forty-plus children in a class. None of the kids could read. It was my job to set individual goals and get them on the way to success in reading as well as all the other curriculum areas. The poor kids. Because they were isolated, everyone in the school thought they were dumb. Even some of the teachers would say to someone in their class who was lazy, 'If you don't watch out, I'll put you in the Oppo Grade.'

Despite my efforts to lift the perception in the school, no one would play with the Opportunity Class students. They hung around the classroom door at

GREAT BOOKS FOR RELUCTANT READERS

Captain Underpants and the Wrath of the Wicked Wedgie Woman
Dav Pilkey

Jiggy McCue titles
Michael Lawrence

Violet and the Mean and Rotten Pirates
Richard Hamilton, Sam Hearn (illus.)

The True Story of the 3 Little Pigs!
Jon Scieszka and Lane Smith

Loudmouth Louis
Anne Fine

My Mum's Going to Explode
Jeremy Strong

Wicked!
Paul Jennings and Morris Gleitzman

How to Eat Fried Worms
Thomas Rockwell, Emily A. McCully

Asterix and Obelix All at Sea
Albert Uderzo

See also p. 47

lunchtime waiting to get back inside where they would be safe from the taunts of kids in the regular classes. Their self-esteem was at rock bottom. Of course in these more enlightened times schools and teachers would not let such a situation exist.

But my experience has always made me sensitive about withdrawal programs. If done correctly, individual tuition programs can be an enormous help to children who are struggling with reading. These programs are sometimes the only answer for the most difficult learning problems. But they can be expensive in time and money. A teacher may only manage four students in half a day. And the danger of stigma is ever present unless the staff are very careful.

Some schools withdraw the best students as well as those who are behind. In this way, withdrawal is not associated with under-achievement. Parents who attend schools to help with reading can often give individual tuition so that every student receives it. This frees the teacher to work with kids who are struggling.

If you have an older child who can't read, please don't blame yourself. There are a multitude of psychological, emotional, social and physical issues which can be involved. Every parent has children with problems of one sort or another. Families which appear perfect are illusions. There is no such thing as a perfect parent or a perfect child.

Children who reach the age of twelve or thirteen and hate reading are a particular worry. They have fallen through the net and now pose a major challenge. For these kids all of the principles surrounding keeping reading fun are particularly important. These kids (more often boys) need to be reached through their interests. It is time to bring out the big guns. And take a dive into the culture of childhood. On page 180 is my recommended list for hard-core book-haters. Be warned – you may be entering poo territory.

If you employ the strategies in this book and keep everything happy and enjoyable, you will have a very good chance of finding your son or daughter lying on the bed, engrossed in a story and not wanting to be disturbed.

This *is* what it is all about.

11

Computers

The computer will always be a tool
and never a parent

IN THIS CHAPTER

* I love computers. And I hate them.
* Computer access is becoming a measure of advantage.
* The web has countless possibilities.
* Author websites are great sources of information.
* Sending and receiving emails are good reading activities.
* Computers are particularly useful in research.
* A program cannot replace a parent.

W e can't live without computers. They are indispensable in a modern society in the same way as electricity or cars. I own five computers – three in my office, which I share with my secretary. I have another at home and a laptop.

I love them. And I hate them. The bad aspects relate mainly to the pace at which I am forced to work. Every day I get screens full of e-mails which have to be answered. I will send off this section of my book that I am writing now and my editor will receive it within seconds. There is no pausing for reflection while the mail snails its way to Penguin. The illustrations and cartoons for my books reach me almost before the artist's paint is dry. Go, go, go. I can produce twice as much in half the time. This frenetic pace is relentless. I am not sure that it increases my quality of life.

Increasingly, there are research reports indicating that children who do not have computers or web access are disadvantaged educationally. Computer access is becoming a socio-economic indicator of advantage in the same way that ownership of books once was.

But they are so useful. For example – my editor thought that the anecdote about *ghote* spelling *fish* in Chapter 7 should be attributed to George Bernard Shaw. In no time at all she has e-mailed me a full account taken from the web which explains that Shaw heard the story from an unknown colleague. Once I would have spent half a day in the library sorting this out. A book such as *The Reading Bug* has hundreds of facts which need to be confirmed or researched. The saving in time and effort is incredible.

The illustrations for *Rascal the Dragon* were all created, delivered and adjusted electronically.

Getting the most out of it

As I have mentioned already, I have reservations about the ability of computers to tell stories. But I can hardly object to children using them in the same way I do myself.

The World Wide Web is a wonderful research tool. It involves reading and writing and much fun. Sending and receiving e-mails is as legitimate as writing letters and much quicker. So let's make the best of it.

While I am writing this in my office, an eleven-year-old is filling in a day of the school holidays. He is not reading one of the hundreds of children's books I have here. He is playing a game called *Neopets* (neopets.com) on my secretary's computer. He has to adopt one of the little pets on the screen and look after it over a period of days. All the instructions about food and environmental needs are given in writing accompanied by a drawing of the pet which he has printed out. He can choose various alternatives and gain a score for his diligence. He compares this with the progress made by one of his mates.

It is reading. It is fun. And there is nothing wrong with it.

I myself have a web page (www.pauljennings.com). Most published writers do. Children can research their favourite authors and books. These sites are great sources of information for assignments or hobbies. There are sites for every possible interest ranging from hot-rods to hot-houses. If you are interested in something it is on the web.

Most problems with computers relate to their over-use, particularly when a child becomes hooked on violent, mindless or trivial games. Sitting blasting away at computerised enemies can become addictive. There is also an element of cruelty involved in some of the games.

I recall playing a virtual reality program with a friend of mine in an amusement arcade. Keith and I have known each other for years and have enjoyed racing cars together. For the game we donned special gloves, shoes, glasses and helmets and could move around on a small platform. We could view a computerised image of each other inside the helmets and we appeared to be moving around inside a huge building. We had guns to shoot at each other. We could sneak around and ambush the other person. The gunshots were loud and realistic. An element of fear and guilt crept in. Neither of us could continue with the set task of annihilating a friend. Shooting someone else for fun was not enjoyable. Why was I trying to kill Keith? It was not the same thing as beating him on the racetrack.

Okay, it was just cops and robbers. Or was it? And anyway, what did this particular game have to offer in the first place? Shooting people was never a good idea.

There are thousands of useful computer games and activities which can be purchased and many of them involve reading and associated skills. Like most things they also involve the parents, who must help choose the programs and supervise their use.

Word-processing, publishing and printing programs have obvious value. Talking books (CD-ROMs where a narrator reads the text) are a good idea, although my own observation tells me that children who will happily sit on a parent's knee and listen to a story do not find the same tale compelling when a narrator reads the print on a screen. They do, however, enjoy clicking on the pictures and making them move.

Computer games and puzzles are lots of fun and so are creative games which involve thinking.

The web has countless possibilities related to real life. Going on a holiday? Your child can immediately access every resort from Tasmania to Toronto. There are pictures and prices. Let the kids do the initial research. It is great motivated reading. It is meaningful reading. And it contains not a moment of pain.

Not a substitute

Computers are an aid to learning and a great tool for writing. They are particularly useful in research and have largely supplanted encyclopedias and other types of reference books. They are not a substitute for parents and teachers. One of the saddest sights I have ever seen was a school where the whole curriculum was based on programmed learning. Every child sat at a computer where they ingested facts. Then they responded to questions which were marked by the computer. Depending on the result, they moved on to the next level or sideways to a remedial level. These schemes, which are based on learning theory developed by B.F. Skinner, use rewards (reinforcement) as motivation.

Love, however, cannot be defined as a reinforcement. It is present when children fail as well as when they succeed. It only works if it is unconditional. It is bestowed irrespective of the result. If we want happiness to be one of the results of learning we must also include love in our methods. This is why the computer will always be a tool and never a teacher. And why a program cannot replace a parent.

12

A Sunlit Valley

Shedding a few tears on the journey

IN THIS CHAPTER

∗ Some things to think about when choosing books for children.

∗ It is the unspoken that is unspeakable.

∗ Laughing at our fears is one of the great ways to gain power over them.

∗ The ability to put ourselves in the place of another makes us truly human.

∗ Hope and joy must be the gifts on the final page of our story.

Ultimately, the choice of what is suitable for your child is up to you. I have mentioned a lot of wonderful children's books in the preceding chapters. But we are not all going to like the same thing. We are not even going to agree on what is good or proper. No two people will have the same definition of fine writing. Every year when children's literary awards are announced, there is controversy. In my opinion it is healthy that there is division over what constitutes a good book.

But it can be confusing to parents. How can you judge what is good? Well, let's start with something on which we all agree. We want our children to grow up to be happy people.

Happiness, however, is not achieved without struggle. It has to be fought for. And it is fleeting. No one exists in a state of complete bliss. Life certainly has many problems. We do not do our children a favour if we pretend that everything is easy. We cannot shelter them from the truth that there is pain, hardship and loss in life. Not knowing what is the right thing to do is a daily experience. Being unsure is part of being human.

Dangerous writing

I have to say that I am attracted to people who are not sure of themselves. Those who have no self-doubt may have a role to play in our society but I find them unsettling.

I am always riddled with doubt about my stories. I frequently phone my editor and recall a book at the last minute before it goes to the printer in order to take out a word or phrase that may be offensive or harmful. The last thing I would want to do is make a child unhappy. It is a constant worry – is anything I have written likely to cause pain? Have I gone too far?

When we write children's books containing tension, both the writer and the reader are close to the edge. The writer may step over the edge by writing something harmful. The child will fall over if they are harmed. But we cannot deny that the edge is there. A child must look over it and a writer must walk close to it. There has to be some form of tension in a story. But how much?

Anyone who writes funny books like I do is writing and living very close to the edge. Humour dates very quickly. Once a joke is known one does not want to hear it again. Surprise is a critical factor. So is danger.

A punchline is a dangerous moment. If it offends, no one will laugh – particularly the critics. But if there is no danger, no one will laugh either. It is not just an edge – it is a knife-edge that has to be walked. One can never get it wrong.

I don't receive many letters of complaint. But I did get a nasty shock in the mail one day not long ago. The writer referred to a short story called 'Without a Shirt' (*Unreal*)

which I thought was very funny. It was about a boy
and his mother who lived in a house in the middle of a
cemetery. The setting was a real house from my home
town of Warrnambool. Many years before the boy was
born his grandfather had drowned and was buried in the
cemetery. The boy had an imaginary speech disorder in
which he had to say 'without a shirt' at the end of every
sentence. 'I am going to give a talk without a shirt.' 'I am
going to school without a shirt,' et cetera.

I subsequently wrote a television script of this story
for 'Round the Twist', a series which has won numerous
awards around the world. I had never received a complaint about this story in seventeen years. Until this
letter.

Dear Mr Jennings,

My children and I have read and liked some of
your books – particularly the Gizmo stories. However,
I have recently come across some disturbing pages
and will no longer use your stories.

One of my children has been reading
your book *Unreal*. I am writing to object about
the content in the short story 'Without a Shirt'.
There are some worrying aspects including
the following:

a The main character's father dies.

b The boy buries his dead cat.

c The single parent family has to live in a house in the middle of the cemetery.

d The destitute mother is on a pension and can't afford to live elsewhere. (Haven't you heard of public housing?)

e You have named the dog Shovel and created a joke by making it dig holes in the cemetery.

f The boy can see all the graves from his bedroom.

g Even though Ben Byron was a heroic figure he was drowned when a sailing ship sank.

After reading seven pages I gave up the story in disgust. The story is totally macabre. I know about children and what is good for them. I am a consultant paediatrician.

Yours sincerely etc.

This letter may seem a little ridiculous but there is a serious issue involved. Writers must not hurt children with their stories. We authors for children should not get too far ahead of community standards or we will fall over the edge. I am talking here about primary-school children, not adolescents. The rules for adolescents are much closer to the rules for adults.

I know, however, that parents and teachers of primary-school children put a trust in me that I will not be offensive when I write. I don't have swearing in my books. And I try not to frighten my readers or present a bleak view of the world.

The paediatrician had a right to express his opinion. And there may be some of you who agree with him.

So what about the proposition that the boy's room with a view was harmful? Is a humorous look at the cemetery offensive? In my home town the graveyard is centrally placed and one can't miss it. Every kid knows where it is and what is in it. The main effect that it has on me is to be grateful that I am still alive and to stop worrying about trivial things and get on with life.

Life renews itself

Should we build a large brick wall around the cemetery and refuse to talk about what is in there? I don't believe so. Happiness is not attained by denying that a lot of life is unpleasant. People do die. Pets pass on. One day Grandad will not be there any more. There *are* orphans who are left on doorsteps. Children know these things.

We wish that they didn't have to face the prospect of death. It's not nice for them.

I remember one day when one of my own children sat playing on my wife's knee, fiddling with the tokens on her charm bracelet. Claire said, 'When I die this bracelet will be yours.' Gemma immediately burst into tears and wailed, 'I don't want you to die.'

I can recall from my own childhood the fear of a parent dying. The prospect is the most appalling thing for a child to contemplate. Particularly for those like the children of migrants who have no supporting family or grandparents and uncles and aunts. My sister and I migrated to Australia from England with only our parents. I used to pray every night that they would not die. There was no one else who loved us.

I will write stories about parents dying. I will not write stories where parents don't love their children. I did once in a tale called 'No Is Yes' (*Quirky Tails*) and have always regretted it. According to the psychotherapist Anthony Storr, abused children will invent parents who love them rather than face the catastrophic truth that they have been abandoned.

Stories like 'Snow White' or 'Hansel and Gretel' may be able to handle this theme because they are fairy tales which invite disbelief. But even these stories make the step-parent, not the parent, the guilty one (now a

no-no for young children's books because step-parents are usually lovely people who have enough problems without being portrayed as wicked).

I avoid themes which present the world as a bleak place. But universal fears are not alleviated by repression. In fact they are made worse. Denial is not the way to peace of mind but just the opposite. Repression is the path to anxiety and neurosis. If the paediatrician doesn't like the humorous approach perhaps he might like to read his son a delightful book called *Bridge to Terabithia* by Katherine Paterson, or *Charlotte's Web* by E.B. White. These authors treat death by ending their tales in hope and the prospect that life renews itself and the grave is not the end of the story.

One of my favourite pieces of poetry is a rhyme by Hugh Mearns. It is chilling.

As I was walking up the stair
I met a man who wasn't there;
He wasn't there again today.
I wish, I wish he'd stay away.

The man on the stair represents our unconscious fears. He is the spectre we dare not confront. And yet, if we do look him full in the face, he will vanish. It is the unspoken that is unspeakable. Laughing at our fears is one of the great ways to gain power over them. Whenever there is a tragedy that strikes our society, jokes will erupt almost immediately. I will have to admit that I do find some of them a bit much but I understand their purpose. Laughing at our mortality is a wonderful way to actually face it. I think a funny story in a graveyard is not only okay but serves a useful purpose. If you can laugh at something you gain power over it. This is why children have rude rhymes at the expense of adults. It gives them a little power.

Charlotte's Web often makes children cry. Some of my stories do too. I once received a letter from a little girl who said, 'Mum was reading me "Ticker" (*Unseen*) in bed and I looked up and she was crying. I said, "What's

wrong with you?" and she said, "Shut up, it's a bloody good story." '

I don't mind people crying over stories. It is the ability to put ourselves in the place of another that makes us truly human. It is because we can use our imagination to be someone else that we can forgo our own pleasures for the benefit of another. It is because people have imagined, that slavery ended. It is because people have imagined, that prisoners of conscience are often freed. It is because people can imagine, that we can hope one day for freedom and justice in the world.

A story can make us be another person in a way that nothing else can. The headlines on television or in the papers may scream the deaths of thousands of people in another land and the catastrophe will not even be mentioned at morning tea. But take a good novel like *Bridge to Terabithia* (Katherine Paterson) and you will see that the tale of the death of one person will make thousands of others cry. A story combined with the imagination of the reader is an incredibly powerful influence for good.

So is it okay for your kids to cry over a story? The answer has to be 'yes'. *The Ugly Duckling* had to be written. Its happy ending is a great comfort to all those who are lonely and lost. The message that there are many others like you is a wonderful relief to children. Every child knows what it is like to be the ugly duckling. Every child knows what it is like to be different.

Stories that don't touch on the fears and problems of life basically are not stories at all because they are not about anything that matters. We are not trying to say that there is no such thing as death or evil. We are not going to pretend that life is without struggle. We are going to offer as well: triumph over tragedy. Effort rewarded. Love winning out.

A story that ends in hope

It is wrong to present the world as a bleak and uncaring place. It is wrong to frighten a child so much that they

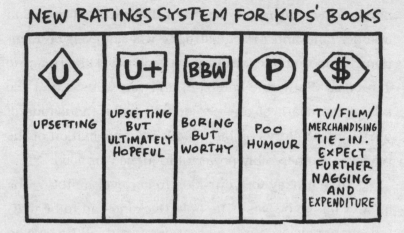

NEW RATINGS SYSTEM FOR KIDS' BOOKS

can't sleep. Hope and joy must be the gifts on the final page of our story.

It is not children's fiction that leads to fear. It is real life, presented on our news bulletins as if murder, mayhem and misery are the only things worth reporting. Many times I have said to myself that I will cancel my morning paper because the daily dose of misery gets me off to a bad start. There are far more fine deeds than self-ish ones in the world. There is more generosity than meanness. There are few people who would not help a child in distress. But this is rarely reported. I sometimes think that 'no news really is good news'.

If someone tears the last page out of a book, you are upset. You haven't had the whole thing. Just a part of it. But this is what television news programs and news-papers do to us all the time. Because stories happen over days, months, years and even generations news bulletins are not able to tell us the happy endings. Every day we see terrible events on the news. A child watching these programs must conclude that the world is a dangerous and terrible place. On the news the little duckling rarely finds its family.

The whole story is not told on the news bulletins because the end of the story is yet to come.

We see a child running down the road away from napalm but at that moment we don't see the young woman she has grown into who is now an articulate defender of peace.

We see fallen walls but not the rebuilt cities.

We see a dead soldier but not the birth of his child who carries his name.

We hear of muggings, robberies and thoughtless stupidity.

GREAT BOOKS THAT MAKE US FEEL BETTER

Pre-school

Willy the Wimp
Anthony Browne

Let's Get a Pup
Bob Graham

Infant

I am Too Absolutely Small for School
Lauren Child

The Velveteen Rabbit
Margery Williams, various illustrated editions

The Owl Who Was Afraid of the Dark
Jill Tomlinson, various illustrated editions

Primary

Charlie's Eye
Dorothy Horgan

Attila, Loolagax and the Eagle
Nichola McAuliffe

Bobby Charlton and the Mountain
Sophie Smiley

So You Want to be the Perfect Family
Josephine Feeney

Secondary

Holes
Louis Sachar

Where in the World
Simon French

But the stories of the millions of caring human beings who go about their business every day are not told.

Am I likely to be mugged in my home town today? It's a possibility but 99.9 per cent of people will never mug anybody. Most people are kind, generous and peaceful.

I believe that the world is slowly becoming a better place. It might not seem this way but things are getting better. In Australia most children are better off today than they were fifty years ago. And they were better off than those fifty years before them. (Although Aboriginal people may beg to differ.) I can't think of an earlier age in which I really would have preferred to live. I believe that we are, however painfully and slowly, moving our way upward. I believe that most humans are caring people. That is the true story.

This is why we write books that end in hope. This is why we don't present a bleak world to our children. But there is pain and suffering in the world. It's how we tell it that is the crucial aspect here.

I could write a story about a spider crawling over someone's toe in such a way that it would scare children for years to come. That would be a terrible thing to do. I could also write about a grandfather's death in such a way as to make it uplifting. The dangerous edge is more often in the telling than in the topic. And the telling depends upon the author's view of the world and of children.

I was recently asked in a radio interview if the world presented to children today is more frightening than when I was young. It's a difficult question. The shadow of World War II and the atomic bomb hung over my generation. But the images were not as graphic as they are on television today. They were not repeated as often. They were not shown on the screen in the terrible realism that they are today. There are frightening things and some of them are happening to children. In Australia, the knowledge that innocent children are locked up in detention centres must be very frightening to our kids.

Books can deal with strong themes in a hopeful way. But in real life the sight of the security fence with children behind it is terrifying to children on both sides of the razor wire. It was reported recently that a young girl in Woomera Detention Centre said to her mother, 'Aren't there any flowers in Australia, Mum?'

I have never written anything as scary as this.

Children's authors can write books about refugees but must do so in a manner that provokes hope and sympathy rather than despair.

As parents this is what we need to look for. Not fear, not denial. Not lies. Not hopelessness. But the prospect of a struggle that is worth the effort. The knowledge that good overcomes evil. That courage can triumph. That life is not a burden but a wonderful gift.

Through stories our children can learn that there is no such thing as a bad nation. Through stories they can share, however momentarily, a few pangs of hunger. Through stories they can see a little of what it is like to belong to a different culture. Through stories they can admire the greatest minds and the bravest souls. Through stories they can escape for a while into the world of laughter. They can fly to the stars. They can ride a broomstick. Or have teeth that glow in the dark.

We all have different views about what is right for children. This is as it should be. As parents we want our kids to be inspired. To be exposed to a little magic. In the process we writers may take them to the edge – but we must never let them fall over. Ultimately, you are the judge of where this point is.

I hope this book helps you guide your children towards reading independence and a love of books. I hope they will have a lot of laughter and joy. But if on this journey your kids shed a few tears as they turn the pages you need not worry. Because you as the parent, together with many caring authors and teachers, will make sure that the children end up in a sunlit valley . . .

where flowers grow.

13

Brilliant Books

Go get them

IN THIS CHAPTER

* Every child is different.
* You are a part-owner of the library.
* Booksellers want us to walk in.
* Other places to get brilliant books.
* The booklists: just a taste of the treats in store.

I remember visiting a student teacher when I was lecturing in literacy studies. She had selected a 'reader' from a well-known formal scheme, and was listening to a little girl read from it. 'Whatever possessed you to choose that book?' I growled. 'We have studied so many fantastic titles for you to select from.'

The student nodded to the child and said, 'She likes it.'

I hung my head and apologised. Every child is different and it reminded me to keep an open mind. A cheap book from the supermarket counter might be what appeals. But there are many other places to consider too.

Bookshops and libraries are the obvious choice for sourcing great books. Some people are intimidated by them and I have often wondered why this is. Libraries tend to be quiet places and in the old days one could not say a word. But librarians love books and stories, which means that most of them are very sensitive to other people's needs. And the children's section of a library usually contains reading corners in which read-alouds, performances and talks by authors and illustrators are often conducted. Most libraries, especially in holidays, make a great (and cheaper) alternative to going to the movies. I always remind myself that, along with every other resident, I am a part owner of the local public library. Some of the books listed in this chapter will go out of print in the future. Others may change publishers. The library is a good place to track down these books.

Changes are also occurring in bookshops. Their aim is to make money by selling books and they really do want us to walk in. Cafe-bookshops are a good development.

Don't hesitate to order in a book that is not in the shop. The bookseller wants to help.

Cheaper alternatives are second-hand bookshops, markets and garage sales. It is possible to pick up some wonderful titles for less than a dollar. Also, don't forget about swapping with friends. Talk about the titles your own children have enjoyed – there is a good chance that other kids will too.

There is a lot of crossover with books. When using these lists, bear in mind that many books will appeal to a very wide age group. The categories here are a guide only. An outstanding book that has been included in the lower-primary category might be enjoyed just as much by an upper-primary-aged reader.

Most of the books listed here are easy to read. More difficult (but still popular) titles are signalled. This is not an exhaustive list but only a taste of the treats in store. Most authors have written many other books and finding the names of them on web pages can be part of the fun.

Treasure-hunting

Once a love of reading is established, the hunt for book treasures will become a part of your children's lives.

Our happy ending is to know that no matter where they go, a child lost in a book will always find their way home.

Books for babies

Babies will respond to colour and shape from the moment they open their eyes. Apparently two dots and a slash on a circle – a face – will always get a reaction. Songs, chants and rhymes are going to be a blessing too.

As Big as a Pig by Allie Busby, SCHOLASTIC
A big chunky board book about being big – or small. Bold, bright illustrations offer lots to talk about.

Baby Faces by Sandra Lousada, MACMILLAN
A good first book with round pages, a rattle, glorious photographs of baby faces and just a few words for the adult to read and talk about.

The Big Red Bus by Judy Hinley, illustrated by William Benedict, WALKER
Wheels on the bus go round . . . into a pothole and the traffic behind must STOP. Big and bright ink-and-gouache illustrations and note the centre-fold.

Boo Barney by Alex Ayliffe, ORCHARD
A strong rhyming text and terrific baby pictures combine to offer a memorable reading experience as the baby moves with action, noise and love through the book.

The Brave Ones by Tony Kerins, WALKER
Polly, Jim, Big Eric, Barker and Birdy are NOT very brave and little Clancy has a big surprise for them. Lovely, chant-like text. Will remind of the famous C.J. Dennis poem **Hist!**

Cleo the Cat by Stella Blackstone and Caroline Mockford, BAREFOOT BOOKS
A rhythmic text and great pictures take readers through the busy day of Cleo from the time she wakes up in the morning up to the moment she falls asleep.

Dear Zoo by Rod Campbell, PUFFIN
Lift-the-flap surprises, minimal text and line, with splashes of primary colour.

First Things First by Charlotte Voake, WALKER
Pictures, rhymes and words combine to reflect a child's first learning experiences.

Guess How Much I Love You? by Sam McBratney, illustrated by Anita Jeram, WALKER
How to measure love? A big theme for the very young. Also in board and other novelty editions.

Hug by Jez Alborough, WALKER
A small and beautiful animal book about hugging and especially about being hugged by the right mother – the challenge for the adult is to read the word 'Hug' in many different voices!

If You're Happy and You Know It illustrated by Annie Kubler, CHILD'S PLAY
A book that results in a jolly, active and noisy experience – just sing the traditional action rhyme to your baby and watch the fun.

I Love You Just the Way You Are by Virginia Miller, WALKER
Bartholomew the bear is having a grumpy day in this warm, beautifully observed board book, and his behaviour absolutely reflects the behaviour of small children.

Kipper's Book of Colours by Mick Inkpen, HODDER
A great introduction to Kipper, a well-loved character often seen on TV. In this one Kipper learns about colours but there are many more titles to choose from.

Let's Go To Bed by Pamela Venus, TAMARIND
Beautiful illustrations of a very real toddler, and a good rhyming text, give this book its child appeal. Babies delight in this well-observed run up to bedtime. Look for other titles about Mimi and her world.

Brilliant Books

My Big Nursery Rhyme Book illustrated by Julie Lacome, WALKER
A huge board book collection of nursery rhymes to dip into – for all young children not just for babies.

My First Board Books, DORLING KINDERSLEY
Bold photos and simple labels help teach each essential first concept, vocabulary and numeracy skills. Bright and colourful.

My Very First Mother Goose edited by Iona Opie, illustrated by Rosemary Wells, WALKER
As a gift to a new baby this will become a family heirloom. Bold design with all the old favourites. Also board-book editions for chewing. Also consider the classic Raymond Briggs' **Mother Goose**.

Number One, Tickle Your Tum by John Prater, BODLEY HEAD
A chunky board book with a counting rhyme and an invitation to join in and wiggle, tickle, jump and giggle with baby.

Owl Babies by Martin Waddell, illustrated by Patrick Benson, WALKER
Mother has gone; will she return? Reassuring and engaging text with illustrations to melt your heart. Also board-book edition.

Peekaboo Friends! by Lucy Su, FRANCES LINCOLN
A very child-friendly, lift-the-flap book with a delightful baby searching for animals on every page – a good introduction to the old game.

Peepo! by Janet and Allan Ahlberg, PUFFIN
Cheeky watercolours of familiar objects and smiling faces. The peephole surprises will delight. Also **The Baby's Catalogue** by the same fabulous duo.

Spot Goes to the Park by Eric Hill, PUFFIN
One in a series of lift-the-flap books featuring this popular dog.

That's Not My Train by Fiona Watt, illustrated by Rachel Wells, USBORNE
A large board book with textures for young fingers to explore and illustrations in bold colours.

Tickle, Tickle by Helen Oxenbury, WALKER
A big board book that fits well across two pairs of knees! The text rhymes and has great 'squelchy' words for the child to respond to. Beautiful illustrations of babies and an invitation to participate in the action.

The Very Hungry Caterpillar by Eric Carle, PUFFIN
Food, growing up, holes to poke, things to count, dramatic collage illustrations that might inspire a budding Matisse, and a chant-like text. A contemporary all-time favourite. Also board-book and other novelty editions.

Weather by Tony Ross, ANDERSEN
One of the many books featuring the Little Princess as she learns about weather – and in other books about life! She's a marvellous, extremely funny character.

Where, Oh Where is Baby Bear? by Debi Gliori, ORCHARD
This lift-the-flap board book encourages the reader, or listener, to join in the search for Baby Bear. There are more good books featuring this warm character.

Who Sank the Boat? by Pamela Allen, PUFFIN
Tension, humour, wit – this has it all. Picture-book perfection with a cumulative text. Read-aloud favourite. Also **My Cat Maisie**.

Wibbly Pig Likes Bananas by Mick Inkpen, HODDER
Every small child should meet this happy character – his amusing antics often reflect those of very young children.

Wiggly Toes illustrated by Sam Williams, MACMILLAN
One of a series of 'buggy buddies' – tiny board books to attach to baby's buggy, cot or highchair. Fun to hold and good to teach babies how books work.

Pre-school books

Mainly picture books still, but pre-schoolers love a bedtime story, so longer texts and poetry can star.

Angelina Ballerina by Katherine Holabird, illustrated by Helen Craig, PUFFIN
Angelina Mouseling dreams of being a world-class ballerina and becomes one. Craig creates a lovable mouse heroine.

Berenstain Bears titles by Stan and Jan Berenstain, RANDOM HOUSE
Family soap opera for the young. Warm and witty situations. Many titles.

Brown Bear, Brown Bear, What Do You See? by Bill Martin Jr, illustrated by Eric Carle, PUFFIN
A predictive pattern to the text which will ensure children feel part of the reading. Collage illustrations which bleed off the page are a knockout. Also in board-book edition.

Can't You Sleep, Little Bear? by Martin Waddell, illustrated by Barbara Firth, WALKER
Little Bear can't sleep because he is afraid of the dark, so Big Bear shows him the splendours of the night. Will move you to tears. A bedtime book so far not bettered, and Firth is at her best with this night-time palette.

The Cat in the Hat by Dr Seuss, COLLINS
Wonderfully, ludicrously inventive as Thing One and Thing Two create domestic havoc. Read aloud or an outstanding read-alone title for beginners. Also **Horton Hatches the Egg**, **Green Eggs and Ham** and many others.

Dig Dig Digging by Margaret Mayo and Alex Ayliffe, ORCHARD
Especially good for boys who love huge diggers and trucks! Good text to join in with.

Dinosaur ROAR! by Paul and Henrietta Stickland, PUFFIN
This book is packed with dinosaurs and its simple, rhyming text makes it an ideal first read – it teaches about opposites as well as dinosaurs.

Dogger by Shirley Hughes, RED FOX
The idea may be familiar – based on the loss of a favourite toy – but the warm story and the pictures make this book an original gem.

Do Monkeys Tweet? by Melanie Walsh, EGMONT
An entertaining book with bold, quite sophisticated illustrations and a text that invites children to make lots of animal noises.

Each Peach Pear Plum by Janet and Allan Ahlberg, PUFFIN
Cumulative I Spy rhyme featuring familiar nursery and fairy-tale characters with peep-through pages.

Eat Your Peas by Kes Gray, illustrated by Nick Sharratt, RED FOX
Mum is wildly extravagant in her bribes to get Daisy to eat her peas. A funny, cumulative picture book.

Elmer by David McKee, ANDERSEN
Good humour and optimism in this very popular story about a gloriously colourful patchwork elephant. Similar themes to **The Rainbow Fish** but quite different approach.

Eloise by Kay Thomson, drawings by Hilary Knight, SIMON & SCHUSTER
Enter the magical world of Eloise in New York's Plaza Hotel. This story entertained the famous – Noël Coward remarked, 'Frankly I adore Eloise' – and Eloise amazes every new generation.

The Enormous Crocodile by Roald Dahl, illustrated by Quentin Blake, PUFFIN
A boastful crocodile sets out to eat a juicy child but justice awaits. Satisfying and funny.

The Elephant and the Bad Baby by Elfrida Vipont, illustrated by Raymond Briggs, PUFFIN
An irresistible text with a naughty baby for a hero and a 'rumpeta, rumpeta' of a chorus to join in with.

Giraffes Can't Dance by Giles Andreae and Guy Parker-Rees, ORCHARD
Giraffes can dance of course – but they do it differently. This is a delight to read aloud and teaches about self-esteem and knowing yourself in the midst of all the fun.

Brilliant Books

The Gruffalo by Julia Donaldson, illustrated by Axel Scheffler, MACMILLAN
A tiny brave mouse walks through a dark wood, a wood inhabited by the hungry Gruffalo. Great language records how the clever mouse tricks the great big Gruffalo.

Hairy Maclary from Donaldson's Diary by Lynley Dodd, PUFFIN
A cumulative, alliterative rhyme with delightful doggy characters. First in a series. Also board and audio editions.

Handa's Surprise by Eileen Browne, WALKER
Glorious images of an African village and a story of a walk and disappearing fruit – the pictures do as much storytelling as the words.

Happy! by Caroline Castle and Sam Childs, HUTCHINSON
Introducing the gorgeous Little Zeb, a small, lovable zebra, on a happy day. Look out for 'Naughty' and a different mood.

How Do I Put It On? by Shigeo Watanabe, illustrated by Yasuo Ohtomo, RED FOX
A simple but very funny book about a young bear trying to get himself dressed. Clear text with questions – and answers that your child will give as soon as he/she gets to know the story.

Hue Boy by Rita Phillips Mitchell and Caroline Binch, PUFFIN
A warm and positive story, set in the Caribbean, about the smallest boy in the village.

I am Too Absolutely Small for School by Lauren Child, ORCHARD
Lola is 'too extremely busy doing important things at home' and simply can't start school. Of course she changes her mind in this hugely creative, very positive book.

I Want My Potty by Tony Ross, ANDERSEN
This book has become a bit of a classic as the Little Princess, introduced in the baby section, grows up and learns how to use her potty. Ross's hilarious illustrations are both entertaining and informative!

Let's Get a Pup by Bob Graham, WALKER
Young Kate wakes 'to Full Summer' knowing this is the day the family should get a pup. They do, but they get old Rosie too. A richly textured picture book about family life, love and renewal characteristic of Graham's magnificent books. Also **Crusher is Coming!**, **Grandad's Magic**, **Rose Meets Mr Wintergarten** and many others.

The Lighthouse Keeper's Lunch by Ronda and David Armitage, SCHOLASTIC
Pesky seagulls upset the orderly life of a lighthouse keeper and his wife.

A Lion in the Meadow by Margaret Mahy, illustrated by Jenny Williams, PUFFIN
An animal fantasy celebrating the imagination and the truth of stories.

Madeline by Ludwig Bemelmans, SCHOLASTIC
'Twelve little girls in two straight lines', words that will now be known from TV, but these stories of a naughty but brave girl date from 1939.

The Man Whose Mother was a Pirate by Margaret Mahy, illustrated by Margaret Chamberlain, PUFFIN
Mother, an ex-pirate, wants to go back to sea. Her conservative but loving son takes her in a wheelbarrow and discovers LIFE.

Mister Magnolia by Quentin Blake, RED FOX
An absolute winner with young children as they join in with the fabulous rhyming text and laugh, in the kindest possible way, at poor Mr Magnolia who has only one boot!

Mr Grumpy's Outing by John Burningham, RED FOX
Cumulative, rhythmic romp on the river featuring Burningham's evocative line-and-wash drawings. Also **Mr Grumpy's Motor Car.**

Mr McGee series by Pamela Allen, PUFFIN
The hilarious adventures of Mr McGee are a huge favourite with children. Crisp, vivid line and colour.

One Duck Stuck by Phyllis Root, illustrated by Jane Chapman, WALKER
A funny story introduces numbers and demands to be read again and again. Very good language to read aloud.

Brilliant Books

Oops! by Colin McNaughton, ANDERSEN/COLLINS
One in a series of twisted traditional tales with clumsy Preston Pig and forgetful Mr Wolf that will thrill children already familiar with the original.

The Paper Bag Princess by Michael Martchenko, illustrated by Robert N. Munsch, ANNICK PRESS
A celebration of a feisty young princess who overturns some fairy-tale standards. Comical illustrations.

Platypus by Chris Riddell, PUFFIN
Like all toddlers, Platypus, a sparky new character, loves collecting things and having adventures.

Pumpkin Soup by Helen Cooper, RANDOM HOUSE
Cat, Squirrel and Duck always make pumpkin soup each day in the same way but ambition overcomes Duck. A riot of fun and a visual delight.

The Rainbow Fish by Marcus Pfister, NORTH-SOUTH BOOKS
A story about sharing. Illustrations include holographs that glitter. Also bath book and other novelty editions.

Red Rockets and Rainbow Jelly by Nick Sharratt and Sue Heap, PUFFIN
A really eye-catching book about two friends, Sue and Nick, who like different colours but still manage to be good friends.

Rosie's Walk by Pat Hutchins, PUFFIN
A Road-Runner plot with a farmyard setting. Stylised drawings and minimal text with much visual fun. Also a board-book edition.

Rumble in the Jungle by Giles Andreae, illustrated by David Wojtowycz, ORCHARD
Splendid collection of animal rhymes set in a vibrantly illustrated jungle – perfect to teach rhyme, rhythm and fun!

Sleep Songs illustrated by Amanda Wallwork, RAGGED BEARS
Two well-loved bedtime songs – **Twinkle Twinkle Little Star** and **Golden Slumbers** – to share after the noise of some of the other recommended titles. Stunning to look at.

The Snowman by Raymond Briggs, PUFFIN
Wordless comic book. Defines the saying, 'every picture tells a story' in a tale of friendship and joy.

Splash! by Flora McDonnell, WALKER (Available from MANTRA in many languages)
A vibrant book that takes us to a sunnier land and tells about the effect of heat on animals and the wonder of water. Lots of repetition – and splashes to join in with.

The Tale of Peter Rabbit by Beatrix Potter, FREDERICK WARNE
The first and most famous of a series of small, exquisitely illustrated books featuring English animals. Read aloud.

Thomas the Tank Engine series by Rev. W. Awdry, EGMONT
A favourite, especially with lovers of trains. In numerous variations and editions.

We're Going on a Bear Hunt by Michael Rosen, illustrated by Helen Oxenbury, WALKER
A family adventure told in a chant-like text, perfect for reading aloud, with delightful wintry illustrations. Also in board and audio editions.

What on Earth Can it Be? by Roger McGough, illustrated by Lydia Monks, PUFFIN
Nonsensical questions precede die-cut pages which give a peek at the possible answer. Wonderful rhymes from this famous poet. Also **Sky in the Pie**.

Where the Wild Things Are by Maurice Sendak, RANDOM HOUSE
A 'wild boy' sulking in his bedroom finds monster companions in an imaginary place and comes to terms with his own aggression.

Where's My Teddy? by Jez Alborough, WALKER
A bear, a boy, and their teddies meet in the woods. Bold in telling and illustration, all books by this author are read-aloud hits. Also **There's Something at the Letter Box**.

Willy the Wimp by Anthony Browne, WALKER
Willy, an undersized weakling bullied by other gorillas, one day sees an advertisement he thinks will help. Surreal illustrations and quirky humour characterise Browne's now famous books. See also his **Hansel and Gretel**, a visual puzzle. Also **Gorilla**.

Non-fiction

Gentle Giant Octopus by Karen Wallace, WALKER
This dramatic account of the lifecycle of an amazing marine creature presents information in such a way as to make it unforgettable.

Puppy Love by Dick King-Smith, illustrated by Anita Jeram, WALKER
A feast of puppies small and big by the author of **Babe** who writes a true tale of all the dogs in his life.

Rain by Manya Stojic, CHRYSALIS BOOKS
This visually stunning book is a joy to read aloud and teaches a great deal about the importance of rain.

Infant (Years 1 & 2)

By this age, some children will want to read by themselves. Finding the right beginner book that will lead them to reading independence is important. Fortunately there are many series just designed for this age group and some outstanding classic books. All make great read-alouds or books to share.

Beware of Boys by Tony Blundell, PUFFIN
A very funny story in which a small boy gets the better of a wolf; a terrific modern fairy tale. Look out for **Beware of Girls** too.

Cats Sleep Anywhere by Eleanor Farjeon, illustrated by Anne Mortimer, FRANCES LINCOLN
An old favourite that manages to appeal to readers of all ages as the images created by poem and pictures really linger in the mind.

Chicken, Chips and Peas by Allan Ahlberg, illustrated by Andre Amstutz,
PUFFIN
With echoes of old animal fables this series confirms Ahlberg's remarkable abilities to create witty, rich texts from the simplest of ingredients. Read aloud or read alone.

A Dark, Dark Tale by Ruth Brown, ANDERSEN
The simple rhythmic text teaches children that a very few words can create a powerful atmosphere and that pictures tell stories too. Children love the anticipation and the surprising end.

Flat Stanley by Jeff Brown, illustrated by Tomi Ungerer, EGMONT
Hilarious adventures of Stanley Lambchop flattened by a notice board.

Frog and Toad are Friends by Arnold Lobel, HARPERCOLLINS
Look for this international classic title about an unlikely friendship, and others in the I Can Read series such as **Little Bear** by Else Holmelund Minarik.

Happy Families series by Allan and Janet Ahlberg, PUFFIN
Miss Dirt, Master Track and many others appear in these clever books with tightly controlled narrative, speech balloons and authorial asides. For beginner readers or as a read-aloud picture book.

Honey and Bear by Ursula Dubosarsky, illustrated by Ron Brooks, PUFFIN
Gentle but emotionally vigorous tales to be read aloud or independently.

The Quangle Wangle's Hat by Edward Lear, illustrated by Helen Oxenbury,
MAMMOTH
A wonderful introduction to the writing of Lear as this great illustrator adds to the famous words and draws characters full of movement and imagination.

Sea Cat and Dragon King by Angela Carter, illustrated by Eva Tatcheva,
BLOOMSBURY
Dragon King is lonely although he rules the ocean and he's very plain, and jealous of Sea Cat's beautiful suit knitted by his mother with love. This story, traditional in style, looks at a familiar theme – ugliness being cured by kindness.

Tashi series by Anna Fienberg and Barbara Fienberg, illustrated by Kim Gamble, ALLEN & UNWIN

Stars a diminutive hero who loves to tell stories of bold adventures. Also an audio edition.

The Three Billy Goats Gruff by Vivian French, illustrated by Arthur Robins, WALKER

The well-known story in a version designed to be read by four voices which produces a poetic result AND is a great aid to beginner readers. See others in the Read Me Story Plays series.

Violet and the Mean and Rotten Pirates by Richard Hamilton, illustrated by Sam Hearn, BLOOMSBURY

A bunch of mean and rotten pirates loot an abandoned ship but all they find is a baby. So Violet, Vile for short, is brought up by pirates and her adventures are pure fun.

The Witch's Dog by Frank Rodgers, PUFFIN

Wilf can't see why he shouldn't be a witch's helper just because he happens to be a dog and this lively story proves that he is quite right. Fun, and a book that feels like a serious read!

Lower Primary (Year 3)

A year can make a big difference. From the triumph of reading a **Happy Families** title at six to some attempting, usually with a struggle **Harry Potter and the Philosopher's Stone** at eight years. Still room for the occasional picture book, and puzzles rule.

Aesop's Funky Fables retold by Vivian French, illustrated by Korky Paul, PUFFIN

The famous fables as you've never heard them before, told in modern rap rhythms and wildly illustrated. See also **Funky Tales**, retellings of traditional stories.

Astrid, the Au Pair from Outer Space by Emily Smith, RANDOM HOUSE
Life is very exciting for Harry and Fred when a new au pair, an alien, arrives to look after them.

The BFG by Roald Dahl, illustrations by Quentin Blake, PUFFIN
A tale of happy-ever-after in a fantasy world of cruel, and one very kind, giants.

Captain Abdul's Pirate School by Colin McNaughton, WALKER
Life at a pirate school is full of surprises – there's never a dull moment in this book that entertains through both words and pictures.

Charlotte's Web by E. B. White, illustrated by Garth Williams, PUFFIN
First Fern, and then a spider called Charlotte, save Wilbur, a little pig, from death. Elegant prose, insightful and moving. A read-aloud for this age, to read alone later.

Cinderboy by Laurence Anholt, illustrated by Arthur Robins, ORCHARD
Cinderella as you've never heard it before – just one of a terrific series of **Seriously Silly Stories** based on traditional tales.

Brilliant Books

The Emperor's New Clothes by Hans Christian Andersen, WALKER
A tale where the child is the hero amongst some very silly adults. Recommend the Naomi Lewis translation with illustrations set in 1913 Europe by Angela Barrett.

Fox by Margaret Wild, illustrated by Ron Brooks, ALLEN & UNWIN
A picture book modern fable in an Australian bush setting that is a remarkable artistic and literary achievement.

George Speaks by Dick King-Smith, PUFFIN
This hilarious story tells of a baby who can talk by the time he's four weeks old – a good introduction to this popular author.

Grimm's Fairy Tales by Jacob and Wilhelm Grimm, illustrated by George Cruikshank, PUFFIN
Includes the classic tales, 'Hansel and Gretel', 'Rumpelstiltskin', 'The Twelve Dancing Princesses' and more. Read aloud.

How to Live Forever by Colin Thompson, RED FOX
A picture book for all ages and one to look at again and again. The story is set in a library crammed full with every book that has ever been written – the idea and the execution are both brilliant.

The Iron Man by Ted Hughes, FABER
A myth, a fairy tale, a story – a hard book to categorise – the language is wonderful and the whole reads like a long, very dramatic poem and is never forgotten.

It's Not My Fault! by Bel Mooney, EGMONT
One of a series of books about Kitty and her growing-up. The stories are short and accessible and reflect the lives of many young children.

John Brown, Rose and the Midnight Cat by Jenny Wagner, illustrated by Ron Brooks, PUFFIN
A complex picture book about companionship, ageing and death that lends itself to a number of interpretations but which can be enjoyed by the very young as well as challenge older readers.

The Jolly Postman by Janet and Allan Ahlberg, PUFFIN
A book packed with intriguing letters and cards for the Jolly Postman to deliver to well-known fairytale characters.

Lizzie Zipmouth by Jacqueline Wilson, RANDOM HOUSE
To talk or not to talk is the dilemma in this terrific little book. It's great for young readers to meet the work of this popular author.

Mr Majeika by Humphrey Carpenter, PUFFIN
Class 3 are lucky enough to have a magician turned teacher in charge and so life is never dull. There are many Mr Majeika stories to look out for.

The Magic Finger by Roald Dahl, PUFFIN
One of the first Dahl books that children enjoy independently – the magic in it really makes them laugh.

The Mousehole Cat by Antonia Barber, illustrated by Nicola Bailey, WALKER
Set in Cornwall, this is the story of a fisherman and his cat who brave a great storm to save their village – rhythmic text and wonderful illustrations.

Old Tom series by Leigh Hobbs, LITTLE HARE
Comic adventures of a wicked cat with wild illustrations and minimal text.

The Owl Tree by Jenny Nimmo, illustrated by Anthony Lewis, WALKER
A fight to save a tree, home to a barn owl, involves an element of magic.

The Owl Who Was Afraid of the Dark by Jill Tomlinson, VARIOUS ILLUSTRATED EDITIONS
Plop, a small barn owl, is afraid of the dark. He overcomes fear through research. Available as a short novel or as a picture book.

Please Mrs Butler by Allan Ahlberg, PUFFIN
Children love poetry at this stage and it's sometimes very liberating to be able to dip into a book instead of reading it all. These school poems are perfectly observed and children relate to them with real pleasure.

Brilliant Books

Six Storey House by Geraldine McCaughrean, HODDER
Tall, thin and dusty Six Storey House stands in its garden and grows older. It is no longer owned by one family but is separated into six flats – the book tells the entertaining stories of the occupants.

Princess Smartypants by Babette Cole, PUFFIN
Fun parody of fairy-tale plots with a gender focus.

Squids Will be Squids by Jon Scieszka and Lane Smith, PUFFIN
More fables – this time the fables Aesop might have written if he had been alive today. Fun and irreverent.

The Tree House by Gillian Cross, OXFORD
The building of a tree house is delayed when dad has to go abroad and all that is needed to finish this adventurous family story, is dad's return.

The True Story of The Three Little Pigs by Jon Scieszka and Lane Smith, PUFFIN
It was all a mistake. A. Wolf was just trying to borrow a cup of sugar; he has been sadly misunderstood. Look out for other hilarious reinterpretations of traditional tales by this team.

The Ugly Duckling by Hans Christian Andersen
Available in many editions. The translation by L.W. Kingsland, published by Oxford University Press is very fine. Special for all ages. Read aloud. Also The Little Match Girl and many others.

The Velveteen Rabbit by Margery Williams, VARIOUS ILLUSTRATED EDITIONS
A rabbit left with other toys in the nursery learns how he could become real through love. A poignant and sentimental illustrated story, but so very appealing.

The Whale's Song by Dyan Sheldon, RANDOM HOUSE
Fantasy with a conservation theme. Outstanding illustrations awarded the Kate Greenaway Medal.

Where the Forest Meets the Sea by Jeannie Baker, WALKER
A poignant tale of environmental change with remarkable collage constructions illustrating the story.

Winnie-the-Pooh by A. A. Milne, illustrated by E. H. Shepard, METHUEN
Enchanting tales of the bear with a very little brain and his friends in the Hundred Acre Wood. Perfect read aloud for bedtime. Sequel The House at Pooh Corner. Many editions including board and audio books.

Where's Wally? by Martin Handford, WALKER
Find the hidden Wally on each page. This is entertaining for older children and adults too.

The Worst Witch by Jill Murphy, PUFFIN
The first in a series of adventures of Mildred Hubble as she attends Miss Cackle's Academy of Witches — the kind of book that confident readers just can't put down.

Non-fiction

Dogs' Night by Meredith Hooper and Alan Curless, FRANCES LINCOLN
A mixture of fiction and non-fiction as the book takes us into the National Gallery to see the dogs in pictures come out at night – great until one night they go back into the wrong pictures. A wonderful way to learn about art.

From Zero to Ten The Story of Numbers by Vivian French and Ross Collins, ZERO TO TEN
One of the most exciting books about number ever published – it manages to be fun and informative throughout as it invites readers to think about how it all began.

The Magic School Bus series, by Joanna Cole, illustrated by Bruce Degen, SCHOLASTIC
Explores non-fiction in a picture-book format. Also suitable for upper primary.

River Story by Meredith Hooper, Illustrated by Bee Willey, WALKER
The story of a river from its birth in the mountains and on its long journey to the sea. Really good text and pictures.

Middle Primary (Years 4 & 5)

Needed now are books that look 'grown-up'. So many old favourites to turn to such as **Biggles, The Wind in the Willows, Anne of Green Gables** or **Little Women** and famous fantasy series like **The Borrowers** or E. Nesbit's stories from Victorian times. Exotic worlds to encounter as well as contemporary stories.

Alice's Adventures in Wonderland by Lewis Carroll, illustrated by John Tenniel
THE children's book classic notable for its use of word play and for the introduction of characters which are part of our literary heritage. Scary, strange and unforgettable. Read aloud.

Aquamarine by Alice Hoffman, EGMONT
Two friends have one last summer together before one moves to a new home on the other side of the country – it's a magical summer of dreams and friendship.

Asterix series by René Goscinny, illustrated by Albert Uderzo, ORION
Short Asterix and mighty Obelix are a classic mismatch made in heaven. Despite or maybe because of Latin word games, readers love these classic graphic stories with lots of fighting and food.

Blitzed by Robert Swindells, TRANSWORLD
An exciting time-slip story in which a boy on a school trip suddenly finds himself back in the time of World War II.

Captain Underpants series by Dav Pilkey, SCHOLASTIC
Potty, rather than toilet, humour. An infant superhero fights the perilous plotting of Professor Poopypants and other villains. Lots of graphics.

A Caribbean Dozen by John Agard and Grace Nichols, WALKER
A brilliant book of poetry by thirteen Caribbean poets – the book resonates with rhythms and images of the islands.

Farm Boy by Michael Morpurgo, illustrated by Michael Foreman, COLLINS
A lovely cross-generational story. Grandpa has a terrible secret. He can't read or write.

How to Eat Fried Worms by Thomas Rockwell, illustrated by Emily A. McCully, ORCHARD
A short novel with absolutely repulsive situations. Sure to be enjoyed. Also an audio edition.

The Hundred and One Dalmatians by Dodie Smith, EGMONT
This story, and now the films, are part of the necessary things of childhood – great to share or to read independently.

It Was a Dark and Stormy Night by Janet and Allan Ahlberg, PUFFIN
A story within a story follows this well-known opening line – the humour is really appreciated by confident readers.

Justin and the Demon Drop Kick by Bernard Ashley, PUFFIN
Humour, football and school combine to make this story, and others in the series, a pleasure – especially for boys.

The Killer Underpants by Michael Laurence, ORCHARD
One of a series of seriously funny stories featuring the sometimes misunderstood Jiggy McCue – great books to relax with.

Lily Quench series by Natalie Jane Prior, PUFFIN
Lily comes from a family of dragon-slayers but finds a dragon is her best ally in troubled times.

The Magic Faraway Tree by Enid Blyton, EGMONT
The most commercially successful and controversial children's author ever. Her books continue to be popular despite disapproval and even bans. This is one title of many and often mentioned as a favourite.

The Magician of Samarkand by Alan Temperley, MACMILLAN
A magical and quite traditional adventure story in which good battles against evil and saves the day.

Brilliant Books

Matilda by Roald Dahl, illustrated by Quentin Blake, PUFFIN
Dahl has generated almost as much controversy as Blyton because he appeals to childhood instincts – good and bad – but he is a much more skilled writer. Most of his books end with children triumphing over injustice and **Matilda** is one of the most satisfying in this respect. See also his autobiography **Boy**.

Midnight for Charlie Bone by Jenny Nimmo, EGMONT
The first in a fantasy trilogy featuring Charlie Bone the boy who looks at photographs and hears the people in them speak. Missing parents, revolting relatives, a stolen baby, an ancient and peculiar school – and magic – make this book a winner.

Mr William Shakespeare's Plays by Marcia Williams, WALKER
A joyous introduction to the Bard in graphic format.

The Orchard Book of Greek Myths retold by Geraldine McCaughrean, illustrated by Emma Chichester Clark, ORCHARD
A good-to-look-at, very readable collection of these great tales. Remember, children still enjoy being read to and try them with Pandora's story.

The Phantom Tollbooth by Norton Juster, illustrated by Jules Feiffer, COLLINS
Light-as-air wordplay and wit in this comic fantasy novel.

The Quigleys by Simon Mason, TRANSWORLD
A very funny slice of family life in the Quigley household – more stories to come.

The Railway Children by E. Nesbit, PUFFIN
A really life-affirming family story as a mother and her children learn, with the help of the wonderful Mr Perks the Station Master, to live in the country and wait for father's return.

Redwall series by Brian Jacques, RANDOM HOUSE/PUFFIN
Heroes and heroines who are all forest animals, epic battles, feasting and storytelling. This fantasy series has many fans.

The Secret Garden by Frances Hodgson Burnett, PUFFIN
The growth of friendship and shared dreams between two lonely children is at the heart of this beautifully told story.

The Sheep-Pig by Dick King-Smith, PUFFIN
One of the most endearing animal stories ever – and an adventure and a near-fatal misunderstanding add edge to the gentle humour.

Snow White in New York by Fiona French, OXFORD
The classic Snow White story set in upper-class New York in the 1920s.

Storm Boy by Colin Thiele, BBC
A moving and inspiring story about a boy, his father and a pelican, set on the Coorong coast in South Australia. Also basis of a much-admired film. Many editions, some illustrated. Also an audio edition.

Tintin series by Hergé, MAMMOTH
Tintin and his dog companion, Snowy, always get things right, unlike irascible Captain Haddock. Classic graphic tales of derring-do.

You Tell Me by Roger McGough and Michael Rosen, PUFFIN
A collection of humorous poems by two of our most popular contemporary poets – a good book to dip into.

Varjak Paw by S. F. Said, DAVID FICKLING
The memorable story of a Mesopotamian Blue kitten who goes out into the world to discover the Way, a kind of martial art for cats. Exciting and very unusual.

Way Home by Libby Hathorn and Gregory Rogers, ANDERSEN
A dramatic, beautifully designed picture book about a homeless boy in the city. A very grown-up theme and a reminder that children still enjoy short texts although they're able to manage longer novels.

Weslandia by Paul Fleischman, illustrated by Kevin Hawkes, WALKER
Wesley's parents worry he is too nerdish but in the holidays he creates his very own civilisation in the backyard and wins over the bullies. Glorious colour and invention in this picture book for older readers.

Wicked! by Paul Jennings and Morris Gleitzman, PUFFIN
A bizarre adventure story. See also **Deadly**.

The Wind in the Willows by Kenneth Grahame
Many editions of this exceptional book, likely to be one of the great story experiences of a child, especially if read aloud. For the latter try a selected edition like **The Adventures of Mr Toad** illustrated by Inga Moore (Walker).

Non-Fiction

Coming to England by Floella Benjamin, PUFFIN
Floella's autobiography tells of leaving Trinidad and coming to live in England where she felt she had to be twice as good as anyone else to survive.

Kings and Queens by Tony Robinson, RED FOX
An irreverent look at the monarchs who've given us so much to talk about over the years – which one was it who died on the toilet?

The Magical Worlds of Harry Potter by David Colbert, PUFFIN
All you ever wanted to know about Harry Potter – the stories behind the stories, the origins of the magical creatures, and much more.

My Story series, SCHOLASTIC
Personal accounts from fictional children who lived during important times or through great historical events – on board the Mayflower, with the Suffragettes, at Waterloo, etc – all good on historical fact and with photographs, maps, etc.

Super.Activ series, HODDER
Informative, up-to-date and popular these books take on a range of subjects – football, basketball, cartooning, etc – and fascinate fans.

Who Built the Pyramid? by Meredith Hooper, illustrated by Robin Heighway-Bury, WALKER
A clever, dramatically illustrated book that questions everything as it takes readers into the world of Ancient Egypt.

Upper Primary/Lower Secondary (Years 6 & 7)

Who can say what direction a child's reading might take at this age? Possibilities from Philip Ardagh to Dickens.

Artemis Fowl series by Eoin Colfer, PUFFIN
Artemis is the villainous hero of this thrilling fantasy featuring some very tough fairies.

The Amazing Maurice and His Educated Rodents by Terry Pratchett, DOUBLEDAY
This novel for young readers set in the Discworld Universe of Pratchett's adult books is a real treat for fans.

Boy Overboard by Morris Gleitzman, PUFFIN
Jamal is a refugee utterly bewildered by the strange treatment he receives in Australia, a place he thought would be a haven.

Bridge to Terabithia by Katherine Paterson, PUFFIN
Always mentioned when people talk of children's classics. A moving tale of death and hope.

The Dark is Rising by Susan Cooper, PUFFIN
The first in a five-book fantasy sequence in which three children find themselves in a terrible battle between good and evil forces.

The Demon Headmaster by Gillian Cross, OXFORD/PUFFIN
There is more to the Headmaster's sea-green eyes than the children realise – his hypnotic powers are at the heart of this and other stories in the series.

Eddie Dickens Trilogy by Philip Ardagh, FABER
Set in a 19th century world of blotchy skin and runaway orphans and packed with mad adventures and crazy jokes.

Brilliant Books

Frindle by Andrew Clements, SIMON & SCHUSTER
One of the best of contemporary school stories as a boy decides to invent a new word – the pen becomes the frindle and the game between the student and the teacher begins.

Goodnight Mister Tom by Michelle Magorian, PUFFIN
The misery of an abused boy evacuated from war-torn London. The relationship with his foster 'father', old Tom, is inspiring and loving. Also an audio edition.

Harry Potter series by J. K. Rowling, BLOOMSBURY
These fantasy novels have turned children's literature on its head. Although lengthy, even struggling readers are keen to tackle Harry's adventures.

Hatchet by Gary Paulsen, PAN MACMILLAN
A heart-stopping adventure. Brian must learn to survive in the wilderness, with only a hatchet to help him. There are sequels.

The Haunting by Margaret Mahy, PUFFIN
Family history and magic combine in a novel that features a much-loved stepmother.

The Hobbit by J.R.R. Tolkien, COLLINS
Bilbo Baggins, fond of hearth and home, becomes a great adventurer. The modest beginnings of what becomes the great saga, **The Lord of the Rings**. Read aloud.

Holes by Louis Sachar, BLOOMSBURY
Lizards, the Wild West, onions and curses – just some of the ingredients in this tall tale. Great read aloud.

How to Train Your Parents by Pete Johnson, TRANSWORLD
Louis wants to be a comedian and he's not at all bad, but when he moves to a new and highly competitive school everything changes. His parents want straight A's and enrol him for extra classes, chess and generally fill his every moment. His friend explains to him that parents must be trained . . .

The Illustrated Mum by Jacqueline Wilson, illustrated by Nick Sharratt, TRANSWORLD
Two girls struggle alone with their mother's extreme behaviour in an effort to avoid 'the Social'. A poignant and unforgettable novel.

The Hitchhiker's Guide to the Galaxy by Douglas Adams, PAN MACMILLAN
'Don't panic' Arthur Dent is told, but what else should he do when the Earth is destroyed to make way for a freeway and all he has left is a bath towel? A crazy science-fiction romp. Also an audio edition.

Journey to the River Sea by Eva Ibbotson, MACMILLAN
Maia is thirteen and an orphan so is delighted to hear that her aunt and uncle who live way down the River Amazon in Brazil, want to give her a home. This is a splendid journey, an adventure story with everything, including a satisfactory ending.

The Lion, the Witch and the Wardrobe by C. S. Lewis, COLLINS
The best title in the Chronicles of Narnia, but despite the increasingly heavy symbolism in the sequels, readers who love this will want to read the rest.

Madame Doubtfire by Anne Fine, PUFFIN
Desperation leads a father, estranged from his family due to divorce proceedings, to pose as a nanny. Very funny, but so real is the character-isation that hearts are touched.

Mighty Fizz Chilla by Philip Ridley, PUFFIN
A fantasy, a fairy tale? A fresh story of anger and a brilliant linking of stories strange and fascinating makes for a good read for boys and girls alike.

Mortal Engines by Philip Reeve, SCHOLASTIC
A fast and furious story of moving worlds, chases and battles with two great heroes to care about.

The Neverending Story by Michael Ende, PUFFIN
Bastian Balthazar Bux discovers the world of Fantastica in an old book and a way to get to the troubled otherworld.

Brilliant Books

Notes from a Liar and Her Dog by Gennifer Choldenko, BLOOMSBURY
A book for all middle children who, like Ant in this book, sometimes think they've ended up in the wrong family. Eventful and exciting from beginning to end.

Saffy's Angel by Hilary McKay, HODDER
A warm and humorous family story in which Saffy is determined to find out about her past.

The Secret Diary of Adrian Mole, Aged 13 and 3/4 by Sue Townsend, PUFFIN
Day by day insight into the turbulent mind of self-absorbed Master A. Mole. Satiric family novel with sequels.

A Series of Unfortunate Events series by Lemony Snicket, EGMONT
The Baudelaire children are orphaned and left in the care of their villainous uncle, Count Olaf. Sophisticated black humour. Also audio editions.

Shadow of the Minotaur by Alan Gibbons, ORION
Virtual reality, Greek myths, worlds that are hard to separate – this is a scary but unmissable book for all computer-crazed children.

The Snow Goose by Paul Gallico, PENGUIN
The relationship between a maimed recluse, a timid girl and an injured goose. Undeniably sentimental and just a bit dated but this modern fairy tale continues to tug at the heart.

So You Want to be the Pefect Family? by Josephine Feeney, OXFORD
The ultimate in makeover as the Rossi family volunteer to be made into the perfect family – and all on TV!

Stormbreaker by Anthony Horowitz, WALKER
A junior version of James Bond, starring Alex Rider, a modern day teenager. Sequels.

The Story Giant, by Brian Patten, illustrated by Chris Riddell, COLLINS
A book of traditional tales from many cultures told to a giant by four children. The Story Giant is dying and his castle is crumbling but he is determined to find the last story for his collection before he goes.

The Sword in the Stone by T.H. White, COLLINS
Still one of the best tellings of the stories of King Arthur – a challenging
but special read.

Thunderwith by Libby Hathorn, HODDER
This Australian family adventure story was made into a popular tele-
movie.

Time Stops for No Mouse by Michael Hoeye, PUFFIN
Adventurous detective tale of an unlikely hero, Hermux Tantamoq, a
watchmaker mouse who is smitten by the beautiful aviatrix Linka
Perflinger and drawn into a mystery. Also **Sands of Time**.

Toad Rage by Morris Gleitzman, PUFFIN
Only Gleitzman could make you love a cane toad. Anxious Limpy tries desperately to become an Olympic mascot to help his species. Also an audio
edition. Also **Toad Heaven**.

Tuck Everlasting by Natalie Babbitt, BLOOMSBURY
A wonderful old-fashioned fairy tale of a family who have found a way to
live forever – this of course causes more problems than we might imagine.

Two Weeks with the Queen by Morris Gleitzman, PUFFIN
A funny and moving story about a boy's efforts to save his seriously ill
brother. Also **Boy Overboard**.

Ug: Boy Genius of the Stone Age by Raymond Briggs, JONATHAN CAPE
This is a picture book for all ages as a clever Stone Age boy begins to think
that perhaps stone trousers and stone duvets are not the most comfort-
able answer to keeping warm. Fun in both text and pictures.

The Wind on Fire Trilogy by William Nicholson, EGMONT
An unusual fantasy that begins with a world in which everything is
decided by tests and continues on to a fabulous journey to find a home-
land. **The Wind Singer** is the first title.

Where in the World by Simon French, LITTLE HARE
A quiet story in which a boy, a talented musician, learns about life and
loss and begins to grow up.

Brilliant Books

A Wizard of Earthsea by Ursula le Guin, illustrated by Ruth Robbins, PUFFIN
The tale of Ged, and the tests he faced before becoming the greatest sorcerer in all Earthsea. The first in a quartet much loved by fantasy buffs.

Wonder Goal! by Michael Foreman, ANDERSEN
The dream so many have of scoring 'that winning goal' can come true. This book is about the universality of football and Foreman's endpapers show sketches of children playing the game in all corners of the world.

Non-fiction

Boy and **Going Solo** by Roald Dahl, PUFFIN
Dahl tells of his childhood and his early working life for Shell in Africa and in the RAF in World War II – he tells of a life so packed that it seems like a story!

Chinese Cinderella by Adeline Yen Mah, PUFFIN
Autobiographical account of the author's childhood. A very sad and moving story with a happy ending.

Diary of a Young Girl by Anne Frank, PUFFIN
Jewish girl Anne Frank kept a secret diary while hiding in an annex during World War II with her family. A vibrant piece of writing, shocking because it is true.

DK Eyewitness Guides by various authors, DORLING KINDERSLEY
Coloured photographs, maps, timelines, diagrams and text boxes combine in these information books on a wide range of subjects.

Gold by Stephen Biesty and Meredith Hooper, HODDER
This sparkling book is really a brief history of the world as it tells the story of gold from the first making of rocks to the time it becomes a pretty chain round the neck of a twenty-first-century person.

Guinness World Records 2003
At the top of the bestseller list, year after year. Now with web references.

My Family and Other Animals by Gerald Durrell, PENGUIN
Gerald's eccentric family move to Corfu to save money. For him, an animal enthusiast, it's like going to heaven.

The Smallpox Slayer by Alan Brown, HODDER
On the 14th May 1796 Edward Jenner infected a boy, James Phipps, with cowpox. So began one of the most useful medical campaigns the world has known – the only one to date that has entirely eradicated a disease. Brown emphasises the basis of scientific enquiry – close observation – as an encouragement to young readers as something they can do in their own lives.

What's the Big Idea? series various authors, HODDER
A good series that looks at the big issues of today. A good starter is **Chaos and Uncertainty** by Mary and John Gribbin – chaos theory made easy!

Secondary (Years 8, 9 & 10)

This age group will be reading an increasing number of adult titles, and the books in this list also have strong adult appeal.

Child X by Lee Weatherly, DAVID FICKLING
The story of a family torn apart when a secret from the past is revealed. Soon the media are camping on their doorstep and life for the daughter, Child X, becomes intolerable – only lightened by the fact that she is playing Lyra in the school production of **Northern Lights**.

The Chocolate War by Robert Cormier, PUFFIN
What can happen when one stands out from the crowd. A tough story, still horribly relevant to our world.

Coraline by Neil Gaiman, BLOOMSBURY
Are you brave enough to go through the secret door? A satisfyingly scary horror fantasy with a wonderfully resourceful heroine and a clever cat.

Brilliant Books

Exodus by Julie Bertagna, MACMILLAN
Set in a future world when global warming is beginning to cause flooding everywhere. Mara's small island is soon at risk so she and her fellow inhabitants set sail for the tower cities they've heard talked about. The journey is desperate and so is the welcome they receive and soon Mara is planning to move on again. A book packed with contemporary resonances.

The Girl from the Sea by James Aldridge, PUFFIN
A dazzling story of undersea treasure, boats, diving, food, danger and summertime freedom set in France in the 1950s.

Grass by C.Z. Nightingale, PUFFIN
A strong contemporary novel looking head-on at the issue of racism today. The book is set in East London where a girl witnesses a terrible attack on an Asian boy. The boy dies in hospital, the girl is warned to keep out of it – what should she do, is she brave enough to do the right thing?

The Haunting of Alaizabel Cray by Chris Wooding, SCHOLASTIC
Set in a rather twisted Victorian London after a war has left the city and its people bruised, shattered and battle-scarred, this book is both thrilling and chilling. There are dangers on the street, none worse than the menacing wych-kin who threaten the survival of humankind.

I Capture the Castle by Dodie Smith, RANDOM HOUSE
The journal of long-suffering but spirited Cassandra Mortmain, living in a castle with her wacky family without a penny to their name. Not written for children but many a teenage girl has adored this book.

If You Come Softly by Jacqueline Woodson, PUFFIN
A gentle, lovely love story that goes wrong. Two fifteen-year-olds, a black boy and a white girl, are in love for the very first time but all is destroyed in a Romeo and Juliet-like way by a terrible act of faith.

Inventing Elliot by Graham Gardner, ORION
Inspired by Orwell's 1984, this book takes a surprising and fresh approach to bullying; it's a strong and rather frightening book because it feels so real.

The Kite Rider by Geraldine McCaughrean, OXFORD

This extraordinary novel is set in the China of Kublai Khan and is the story of a boy whose father dies when a kite ride goes wrong, and who is then determined to save his mother from a forced marriage. It is Haoyou's story, his journey through China and through life, and through it we get just a glimpse of a long-gone, fascinating world.

Lucas by Kevin Brooks, CHICKEN HOUSE

A novel with a strong sense of place that has the reader really present in the story. It's a story of first love, prejudice and violence as resentment and suspicion of a newcomer grow and explode. A second novel from an exciting new writer of young adult fiction.

Massive by Julia Bell, MACMILLAN

Carmen's mother is always on a diet and she spends time with her food-obsessed grandmother. Moving house means no friends and Carmen really misses her dad, in fact life is tough. The book looks at the interaction between emotional and nutritional needs within the context of a strong story.

Northern Lights by Philip Pullman, SCHOLASTIC

First in the His Dark Materials trilogy and the most approachable for young readers. An extraordinary fantasy with great depth of meaning.

101 Poems That Could Save Your Life edited by Daisy Goodwin, COLLINS

An adult book, a collection of poems to dip into and read in times of need – lots of great poetry to choose from.

Sabriel by Garth Nix, COLLINS

An extraordinary other world, unsettling and provocative. First in a trilogy featuring the Abhorsen, a person who sends the dead to their final rest.

To Kill a Mockingbird by Harper Lee, ARROW

A picture of small town life during the Great Depression in the United States – and a tale of great courage and the wickedness of prejudice.

Brilliant Books

You Don't Know Me by David Klass, PUFFIN
This remarkable book is packed with humour, not least as it describes our central character's first date, but it is also a painful book about abuse and insecurity. Powerful writing, stream of consciousness style makes this a novel that is hard to forget.

Witch Child by Celia Rees, BLOOMSBURY
A remarkable book about a seventeenth-century girl accused of witchcraft. Her story, as she escapes to the safety of New England, is one of prejudice, bigotry and struggle. Look also for the follow-up **Sorceress**.

Non-fiction

Down Under by Bill Bryson, BLACK SWAN
Typically cynical but incredibly witty and affectionate, Bill Bryson's travel books are in a class of their own. Descriptions of sociopathic jellyfish, homicidal crocs and toilet-dwelling death spiders make this account of Australia a classic and easy introduction to Bryson. See also **Notes From a Small Island**.

I Know Why the Caged Bird Sings by Maya Angelou, VIRAGO PRESS
A beautifully written, powerfully emotional account of Maya Angelou's childhood as a black female in 1930's Southern America. The warm, flowing, rich voice makes it impossible for the reader not to become wholly engrossed – but do be warned of a harrowing depiction of sexual abuse.

Mao's Last Dancer by Li Cunxin, FUSION PRESS
Through a dance scholarship, a Chinese peasant boy defects to the US, leaving behind the gruelling hardships of Communist China. An exciting and moving book in which East meets West.

Wild Swans: Three Daughters of China by Jung Chang, FLAMINGO
Through the lives of three generations of women, this book tells the story of twentieth-century China. An unforgettable record of hope, friendship and survival through harsh and dramatic revolutions. An eye-opening read.